How to Coach
Football's
Attacking Defenses

Other Books by the Author:

Directory of Football Defenses: Successful Defenses and How to Attack Them, 1969

Winning Play Sequences in Modern Football, 1971

HOW TO COACH FOOTBALL'S ATTACKING DEFENSES

by Drew Tallman

Parker Publishing Co., Inc.
West Nyack, New York

© 1973, *by*

PARKER PUBLISHING COMPANY, INC.

West Nyack, N.Y.

Library of Congress Cataloging in Publication Data

Tallman, Drew.
    How to coach football's attacking defenses.

    1. Football—Defense. 2. Football coaching.
I. Title.
GV951.1.T35   796.33'22   73–5715
ISBN 0-13-403774-X

Printed in the United States of America

How You Can Use This Book

This book gives the football coach ideas, concepts, thoughts, principles and details of different and successful defenses and how to attack, with proper strategy, the varied offenses of today. Every defense must be prepared to attack anywhere along the line of scrimmage. It should be able to strike at all diversified and conceivable blocking schemes as well. There are numerous offensive series that will be faced and combated during an entire season. The defense must be set for power, double options, triple options, sprint-out passes, drop-back passes and many others. The defensive coach and team must know and understand how to attack varied and multiple offenses, or a team that utilizes only one or two series with very few formations.

To attack offenses, a coach must know the intricate details of each offensive play and series. He should understand the principles and details so he can effectively employ his defense to the best advantage possible. The football coach must understand his defense thoroughly also. He should have at his disposal different defensive schemes so he can attack all aspects of offensive play. Strengths and weaknesses of offenses change from week to week due to numerous variables, including personnel, formations, series, plays, etc. The coach must have the defensive tactics to attack these various offenses.

This book not only gives the football coach exact details to today's modern defenses, but it reveals to the coach exactly how to attack these offenses at any instant. The defenses included are the Split-4, Pro-4 and Oklahoma 5-4 Defense. Other defenses are indicated when desirable for the attack. This book illustrates ways and methods of attacking the middle, off-tackle and outside of the offensive line. Fundamentals, techniques, stunt maneuvers, half- and full-line slants are explained and illustrated fully. When the offense is striking the defense in the flat areas, the book shows how to combat such a situation. Similar ideas are indicated for the middle, hook and deep passing zones.

The option game is becoming more and more popular in offenses. This book describes the many methods of not only halting the numerous double options at the offensive end and corner areas, but also the popular triple option as well. The passing game can play havoc for any defensive team, and chapters are included on how to attack the pro passing game as well as sprint-out action. Intricate details of reading and keying with pass coverages versus any passing pattern are shown in detail for the first time in any book. Man-to-man, zones and different combinations of zones with man-to-man, are all clearly illustrated.

Today's football does not mean picking any defense out of the air and hoping it will work. Using the proper stunt or slant at the correct instant with the utilization of good fundamentals and techniques are very important to a successful defense. This only comes about when the coach spends time on strategical ideas that will find success versus certain plays and formations. The different ideas, thoughts, methods, techniques and information presented throughout the book have been used by one team or another with success. Success came when a play was used at the proper instant (involving formations, field position, down and distance, etc.) and not haphazardly called for no reason at all. It is hoped with the numerous principles, concepts, ideas, methods and suggestions presented throughout the book, a coach will be able to attack offenses better. He should know, understand and be able to teach the concepts more successfully to his team also. He should become an excellent and intelligent strategist versus any offense with a proper study of this book.

                                        Drew Tallman

CONTENTS

How You Can Use This Book   9

1. Fielding a Defense That Attacks the Offense 15

   Coach's Utilization of Defenses (15) Eight- and Nine-Man
   Defensive Fronts (16) Attacking Offenses (18) The Coach and
   Defensive Caller (24) Every Defense Has a Purpose (24) No
   Offense Is Perfect (24) The Importance of Scouting (25)
   Strategic Defensive Maneuvers (25)

2. The Eight Most Widely Used Attacking Defenses 27

   Executing the Split-4 Defense (28) Executing the Pro 4-3
   Defense (33) Executing the 5-4 Oklahoma Defense (38)
   Strengths and Weaknesses of Defenses (40) Other Defenses to
   Be Utilized (43)

3. Strengths and Weaknesses of Offensive Sets,
   Formations and Maneuvers 47

   Classification of Offensive Formations (47) Variations of
   Formations (50) Formations with Strengths, Weaknesses and
   Series (57)

4. Attacking the Middle 67

   Attack the Middle with Other Alignments (68) Defensing
   Middle Offensive Maneuvers (71) Attacking the Middle with
   Stunts (77) Angling (Slant and Loop) (84)

5. Attacking Off-Tackle and Outside 87

   Different Offensive Maneuvers (88) Attacking Off-Tackle with
   Other Alignments (90) Attacking Outside with Other Align-
   ments (93) Attacking Off-Tackle Versus Different Offensive
   Maneuvers (96) Attacking Outside Versus Different Offensive
   Maneuvers (102) Attacking the Off-Tackle with Stunts (104)
   Attacking Off-Tackle with the Pro-4 Defense (108) Attacking
   Outside with the Split-4, 5-4 and Pro-4 Defenses (110)
   Attacking Off-Tackle and Outside with Angling Lines (111)

6. Attacking Wide-Outs and Flats 115

   Utilizing a Three- or Four-Deep Secondary (115) Importance
   of Different Coverages (116) Formations and Attacking the

Flats and Wide-Outs (116) Different Offensive Pass Routes in
the Flats (117) Attacking the Wide-Outs and Flats with
Different Defenses (118) Defensive Coverage of a Flanker or
Slot Before the Offensive Snap (120) Defensive Coverage of a
Split End Before the Offensive Snap (126) Disguising Defen-
sive Coverages (128) Attacking the Flat with a Four-Deep
Secondary (129) Attacking the Flat with Three-Deep Rotation
(131) Attacking the Wide-Out Receiver with Three- and
Four-Deep Secondaries (133) Attacking Offensive Pass Routes
(136)

7. **Attacking the Inside Receivers and Hook Areas** 139

The Varied Inside Receivers (140) Linebacker Coverage (142)
Attacking Inside Receivers Coming off the Line of Scrimmage
(143) Defenses for the Inside Game (144) Utilizing Zone
Coverage (146) Man-to-Man Coverage (149) Man-to-Man with
Free Safety Coverage (151) Man-to-Man with Underneath
Zone Coverage (152) Covering the Inside Receivers with
Special Defenses (152)

8. **Attacking the Deep Areas** 155

Attacking the Long Pass (156) Secondary Play (157) Disguis-
ing Defenses (158) Employing the Two-Deep Zone (159) The
Three-Deep Versus the Four-Deep Secondary (159) Four-Deep
Zone Coverage (160) Man-to-Man Defenses (160) Utilizing
Man-to-Man with a Free Safety (160) The Three-One Prevent
Zone (162) Attacking with the Four-One Prevent Zone (163)
Employing the Five Rotate or Invert Coverage (164) Three-
Man Defensive Rushes (164) Attacking with Pressure (165)

9. **Attacking the Triple Option** 167

Stopping the Veer (168) Offensive Plays to Be Controlled
(169) Formation Defenses (170) Importance of Change-Up
(170) Principles of Execution (170) Defenses to Stop the
Triple Option (171) Attacking the Triple Option with the 5-4
Defense (174) Attacking the Triple Option with the Pro-4
Defense (177) Attacking the Triple Option with the Split-4
Defense (180) Defensive Secondary Coverages (183) Attacking
the Outside Veer (184) Other Field Situation Defenses (185)

10. **Attacking the Double Option**. 187

The Swing Option (188) The Split-T Option (189) The Inside
Belly Option (189) The Outside Belly Series (190) The Slant

Option (191) Attacking the Swing Option (191) Attacking the Split-T and Inside Belly Option (194) Attacking the Outside Belly and Slant Option Game (196) Technique of Attacking the Quarterback (198) Technique in Attacking the Pitch Man (199)

11. Attacking the Pro Strategical Passing Game 201

Defensing the Passing Game (202) Reading the Passing Game (203) The Pro Passing Game (204) Formations Employed (204) Disguising Defenses (205) Utilizing the Three- and Four-Deep Coverages (206) Attacking the Pro Passing Game (206) The Triple Option and the Drop-Back Pass (214)

12. Attacking the Sprint- (Roll) Out Pass 217

Defensive Secondary Coverages (217) The Importance of Containment (218) Attacking the Throwback (221) Defensive End Techniques Versus Sprint- or Roll-Out (222)

13. Attacking at the Goal Line 225

Attacking with the 6-5 Goal Line (226) Defensive Pass Coverage from the Goal Line 6-5 (232) Attacking with the Gap-8 (233) Pass Coverage with the Gap-8 Defense (234) Combination of 6-5 and Gap-8 (235)

Index 236

Fielding a Defense
That Attacks the
Offense

In modern football, all too often, coaches desire to know how, when and where to attack a certain defense and its adjustments. This book, however, is one in which the offense will be attacked by today's modern defenses. There are certain defenses that have been and *still are* very successful. The eight-man defensive front, the Split 4-4-3 Even-Diamond; the nine-man front, 4-3-4 Even-Box and the 5-4-2 Odd-Box Defense are utilized to a great extent. These defenses will be explained in exact detail, but it must be remembered that numerous other defenses are successful and will be indicated in attacking offenses. These defenses can include the 5-4 Slant, Eagle-5, Wide-Tackle 6, 6-5 Goal Line and others.

COACH'S UTILIZATION OF DEFENSES

Every coach throughout the country has his own defense (or defenses) that he desires to execute in a season. It is not difficult to have a defense with its adjustments, and various stunts and maneuvers. It is the intelligent coach, however, who knows *how, when* and *where* to employ his defense at the proper moment in a game. This is vitally important. There have been times every year when a football coach said *after* a game how he wished he had thought to utilize a certain aspect of the defense, such as a line maneuver or defensive coverage, to halt an offense.

For example, it is important to attack a certain part of an offense with stunts, but it is necessary to cover other areas of the defense if the offense should execute something different also. If an offensive unit utilizes the triple option and all its variations, the defense must be prepared to stop or slow down the triple option's effectiveness through different defensive movements and adjustments. However, if an offensive team uses the triple option but employs the drop-back passing game to a varied extent as well, a defensive unit must be able to halt both of these offensive series. This must be accomplished in a different manner, because the defense should be prepared for the triple option run-and-pass game, but be in a position to cover the wide receivers and all the various pass patterns a team may utilize in the drop-back pass series. Certain scouting reports will indicate situations where a defense will be used at a particular time or down-and-distance situation. A coach must have at his disposal an entire repertoire of adjustments, stunts and coverages to attack the diversified phases of offensive football.

EIGHT- AND NINE-MAN DEFENSIVE FRONTS

An eight-man defensive front usually consists of a combination of eight defensive linemen and linebackers. With these types of defenses, a three-deep coverage is utilized with various coverages executed. These defenses include the 4-4 Tandem, Split 4-4, 4-3 Monster, 5-4 Monster, 5-3 Defense, Wide-Tackle 6, Gap-8, 7-1 Diamond, etc. Diagram 1-1 illustrates two examples of eight-man fronts.

The eight-man front places emphasis and strength on the running game, because only three defensive secondary men are used against passing. The defense wants to establish pressure on the run and hopes a three deep will cover a four-man release (sometimes five) in the passing game. However, the defense desires to put pressure on the quarterback so he will not have the time to throw the football.

The nine-man front defense utilizes four secondary individuals who can be utilized versus the passing game, and seven defensive

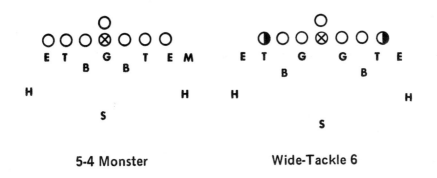

Diagram 1-1

linemen and linebackers to halt the run. However, a four deep is designed to rotate or invert or accomplish other coverages that can support the running game. The outside defensive halfbacks or corner men can rotate forward, or the inside safeties can invert to help support the run. The nine-man front obtained its name because of the seven defensive linemen and linebackers and the utilization of the two outside corner men or halfbacks for the running game. Some of the nine-man front defenses are the 4-3-4, Oklahoma 5-4, Eagle-5, 5-4 Slant, 6-1 Defense, 6-5 Goal Line, 7-4 Defense, etc. Diagram 1-2 indicates two defenses of the nine-man front.

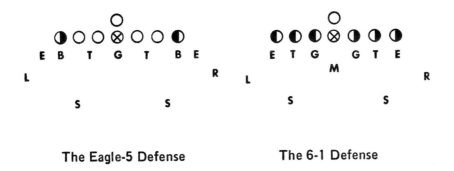

Diagram 1-2

ATTACKING OFFENSES

There are many points to consider when attacking the various offensive systems. The following are some of the thoughts to keep in mind when attacking any running and passing game.

1. Alignments.
2. Proper techniques, fundamentals and execution.
3. Proper keys, reads and coaching points.
4. Individual and team stunts.
5. Angles (slant, loop, etc.).
6. Jumping of defenses.
7. Football knowledge and intelligence.
8. Having all to attack everything.
9. Proper strategy.
10. Attacking all areas.
11. Personnel and defenses.
12. Importance of successful teaching.
13. Defense must be fun.

1. Alignments.

Alignment of a defense is very necessary in stopping any aspect of an offensive unit. A team may utilize the Split 4-4 Defense but is being assaulted up the middle on traps, sneaks, quick-hitting counters, etc. A defensive coach should have in his system an alignment to maneuver too, so he can be effective in slowing or halting the offensive attack. An easy alignment change would be the utilization of the 5-3 Defense. The defensive secondary would not have to alter, and the same would be true for the outside defensive ends and linebackers.

Another example would be a team that utilizes the 5-4 Defense. An offensive team is attacking off-tackle strong but has an excellent passing game also. A simple adjustment, without maneuvering the four-deep secondary, would be the defensive front seven to align in an Eagle-5 Defense. The defensive tackle would slide into the guard-tackle seam while the defensive linebacker aligns on the inside shoulder of the offensive tight end. The linebacker can now assist off-tackle, be in good position to hit the tight end on pass release and cover in the secondary, whether it be man-to-man or zone.

2. Proper Techniques, Fundamentals and Execution.

It is important that a coach teach and drill all the techniques and fundamentals for each position on the defensive unit. While it is necessary to have various defensive sets to attack offenses, it is very noticeable that without good fundamentals and techniques, a team will not be successful. Exact movements, steps, execution, techniques, etc. must be drilled constantly with perfection, in order to find a winning combination. Other defensive alignments and maneuvers can always be added, but only with proper practice time.

3. Proper Keys, Reads and Coaching Points.

It is not necessary to have many keys and reads for defenders. It becomes very confusing when this occurs, and sometimes a coach will lose proper techniques and fundamentals of each defense because of it. Only the simplest reads and keys should be used, and kept to a minimum as much as possible.

Also, a coach should know every coaching point available about each defense he installs. He should understand all the different aspects of techniques, fundamentals, execution, reads, and keys in order for the particular defense to be successful. When an offensive team utilizes a different formation or series, or splits their line more than usual, a defensive coach must have his players react right at the moment to each and every movement the offense makes. Coaching points for each of these movements are necessary for a defense to be successful.

4. Individual and Team Stunts.

Each defense employed must be able to attack the offense if success is being gained in certain areas versus the defense. Diagram 1-3 shows one example. If the 4-4 Split Defense is getting hurt off-tackle, then an individual defensive stunt may be necessary at this point. As indicated, the outside linebacker comes down hard inside on a defensive stunt and attacks anything coming in his direction. The defensive end squeezes inside, but still looks to contain on the corner. The defensive secondary can either play man-to-man or rotate toward the stunt to protect versus the outside run or the vulnerable flat area in the defensive secondary. Team stunts would include almost all defensive front individuals doing the same type of blitz maneuver. The defensive coverage will usually be man-to-man.

*5. Angles (Slant, Loop, Etc.).. *

As was mentioned, with individual and team stunts, different angling lines can be executed to attack an offense. This can be accomplished toward the formation, the field or both. However, it can be utilized any time a defense is being struck in a certain area. According to field position, time of game and what the offense is

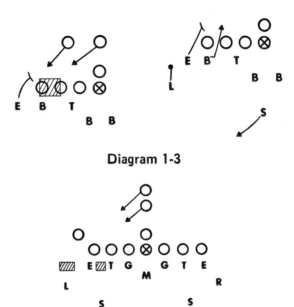

Diagram 1-3

Offense is attacking outside and off-tackle to formation side.

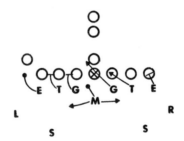

Defense attempts to counterattack by looping and/or slanting in the direction being attacked. The defense is still in good position to cover away from the angling line also.

Diagram 1-4

attempting to accomplish, the defense will employ a slant, loop or combination of both. Diagram 1-4 illustrates an offensive team continually running toward the formation side. The defense, therefore, should slant and/or loop in that particular direction. The linemen to the onside will execute a loop technique while the off-side defensive linemen will use a slant charge. Man-to-man, zone or a combination of coverages can still be utilized.

6. Jumping of Defenses.

Jumping from one defense to another can be very hectic and confusing for the offensive team. The offense is prepared at one instant to block and run versus a defensive alignment, and, at the next moment, must block another defense. If the defense can jump at the right moment, offensive blocking schemes can be disrupted. However, it is important that when jumping is taking place, a defensive player does not have to maneuver far to align in another position. At a certain command (an example would be "move"), he must adjust quickly and easily and be prepared to utilize the proper fundamentals and techniques of the defense jumped to. It should be necessary not to change from a three- to a four-deep secondary also. It is better to jump from an eight-man front to another rather than from a nine-man front to another. There are a few teams that go from a three to a four deep, and vice versa, but a defensive unit must be well-drilled and prepared to know exactly what they are responsible for when accomplishing these changes.

7. Football Knowledge and Intelligence.

One of the most important aspects of the game of football is the ability of the football coach to have an entire knowledge of his own defense and all styles of offenses. He must decide *before* the season begins what his defense (or defenses) can execute in defending certain plays and offenses. Many of his decisions may occur a week prior to the game and possibly right before it begins.

There are only a few coaches today, however, that can think and react while the football game is developing. They are able to employ defensive adjustments and maneuvers versus an offensive attack at the right moment. There have been numerous coaches who have turned their backs away from the game, because they did not know what exactly to do in a given situation. The ability to think and react and have the knowledge to do this intelligently, may hinge on a successful or not so prosperous season.

8. Having All to Attack Everything.

As mentioned previously, a coach must have all at his disposal if he is going to attack offenses successfully. If a coach employs one defense, then he must have every adjustment, maneuver and secondary coverage at his disposal to attack different offenses. If a coach has more than a single defense, he may need less material to cover offensive plays. The coach must be fully prepared to cover various formations with the many series of plays. For example, if a three-deep defensive secondary aligns opposite a flanker, split end and split backfield (Diagram 1-5), then the defense must decide if it can cover four or five receivers out of the backfield with the help of the linebackers. If this cannot be accomplished effectively, the defense may have to revert to a four-deep secondary to cover the passing game. This may have to be accomplished during the course of a ball game also. Therefore, a coach should have this prepared in his mind before the game begins if he is going to take advantage of attacking these offensive maneuvers. Every defensive adjustment must be at the coach's disposal, and all defenders must be able to handle all situations as they occur.

9. Proper Strategy.

It is important for the coach, once he has all the defenses, adjustments and maneuvers, to employ this material at the right moment in the game. Some defenses are not sound versus a good passing attack, especially if the offense can read the defensive movements *after* the snap of the football. The defense must be ready to "read" what the offense is trying to accomplish after the snap of the football and utilize the correct coverage in the secondary and underneath. The "read" defense, however, may not be necessary when the offense needs short yardage, because the defense must get tough and bear down against the offensive attack. Proper defensive strategy depends upon down and distance, field position, time of the ball game, type of offensive sets utilized, the personnel the defense is facing and the different type of offensive series and/or plays that are being used by the offense. Every bit of this comes into the picture at each instant of the game, and the coach must be ready and the ball players prepared to meet each situation.

10. Attacking All Areas.

With proper strategy, the defense must be able to attack all areas of both offensive formations and the field. The defense should have at its disposal the ability to attack outside, off-tackle, off-guard, over the center, flat zones, hook zones, middle zones and the deep areas of the field. The defense should be able to attack one area at once or two areas at a time. The defense may want to stunt outside on the right and off-tackle on the left. With these maneuvers, the defense should have man-to-man, zone or a combination of both, so as to cover the running game at the areas of attack and certain types of pass patterns. The quarterback's ability to throw and the receiver's ability to catch must be considered also.

11. Personnel and Defenses.

Personnel will make a defense strong or weak, sound or

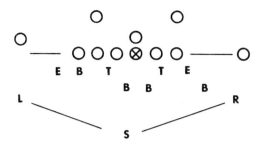

Diagram 1-5

It is more difficult to cover this formation with a three-deep than with a four-spoke secondary. The width of the formation and the depth of the field can cause problems with a three-deep diamond defense. Good rotation of the three defenders is almost impossible without weaknesses occurring. In this case, good linebacker coverage is of necessity.

unsound, against offensive movements. For example, a team with players who are excellent linebackers would do much better if it used a defense which employs many linebacker positions. However, if a coach decides to use another defense with few linebacker alignments, the defense may be weak at the other positions.

12. Importance of Successful Teaching.

It is the material a coach can teach successfully, and have the players execute successfully, that is important. A coach should not attempt to teach something that has not been successful or has not been tried. It is preferable that the coach uses "proven" material he knows best. The better a coach knows and understands his defense, the easier he will be able to teach it, and the better his team will execute it.

13. Defense Must Be Fun.

A necessary element to the game of football, that can be lost to the boys who play, is the idea of fun. Defense, especially, should be made and considered fun for the entire team. At one time it was thought that scoring was the fun of football. However, with the emphasis put on the importance of defense, players can enjoy playing and have fun attempting to initiate tackles and stopping plays. The coach should stress hard work in an attempt to gain success, but he must add a little enjoyment to the game also.

THE COACH AND DEFENSIVE CALLER

The only person who must call defenses and understand them cannot be the coach alone. It is the defensive caller or "quarterback" who must do this also. The defensive play caller should be taught the concept, theory and ideas of the defenses installed. He must be able to call defenses as to formations, series, field position, down and distance, time of game, score, wind, weather, etc., to employ the defense properly and successfully. The coach must constantly teach, train and drill him on all of these important aspects of the game. To accomplish this, the coach and the defensive caller must work together in and out of season to be fully prepared. The coach should have the player think like himself about the strengths and weaknesses of his own defense and the opponent's offense.

EVERY DEFENSE HAS A PURPOSE

A coach should keep in mind that every defense he installs must have a purpose. There are many different defenses with their variations that can either pursue, penetrate, penetrate and pursue, stunt, slant, loop, angle, veer, blitz, fire, etc. However, there should be a sound reason behind employing the defense. Is the defense going to stop the running game, passing attack or both? Does the defense want to stop the offense for no gain, throw a team for a loss or let an offensive team grind it out for a little yardage or small gains, hoping it will not make the big play, such as a long run or a deep pass. Tactical situations will determine greatly when a defense will be utilized. Certain defenses can be used on first down, while others may be utilized on second-, third- and even fourth-down situations. The purposes and objectives of defenses should be known and remembered constantly so they can be employed at the correct and proper instant.

NO OFFENSE IS PERFECT

It should be realized by all coaches, at every level of competition, that no offense in today's modern football is perfect. Some offensive coaches will explain they can read and key before and after the snap of the football and direct their attack according to what the defense executes. This can be done on option plays and reading secondary coverages during the passing game. However, it must be understood that if defenses are taught correctly, and if the offense makes any type of mistake, the ball can easily change hands. Coaches throughout the years have thought of and "invented" new offenses and variations to each. However, of all offenses, not one can provide all the answers. A new offense may materialize one year and cause defenses numerous problems. The defense will eventually catch up to the offense with certain defensive maneuvers and secondary coverages. The field is simply too large for an offense to be "foolproof." Every offense can be attacked in one way or another, and it is up to the football coach to find the best method of attacking each one.

THE IMPORTANCE OF SCOUTING

It is a necessity that the defensive coach utilize scouting. This would include games before the actual play of the opponent and film observations. Most offensive teams have numerous tendencies with formations, field position, offensive plays and passes. The offensive team will have tendencies with certain key personnel, such as a great runner or receiver. These different aspects of the game will determine what a football coach will do with the defensive unit. If an offensive team desires to run continually to certain formations, then the coach can set up his defense to counterattack these tendencies of the offensive team. If a team likes to throw to the left, the secondary coverages can be tactically maneuvered to stop such offensive threats.

STRATEGIC DEFENSIVE MANEUVERS

When attacking an offensive system, the football coach must keep in mind ten different defensive maneuvers or attacking ideas. He may desire to utilize only one, two or three of these points. However, the coach may want to employ all ten methods to attack either one offensive area or an entire offensive system. The following are different methods to attack offenses:

1. Utilize different alignments from the basic defense. For example, if the coach uses the 5-4 Defense he could maneuver to some type of 54 Stack or Tandem look. He could also adjust into a Monster secondary coverage with one of the cornerbacks. The coach,

therefore, can choose from stacking, tandeming, shifting of line-backers and/or linemen, and maneuver into some type of secondary adjustment in the defensive backfield.

2. Employ a new defense. For example, if a coach's defense is the Split-4, he can maneuver into a different defense for a game, such as a Wide-Tackle 6, Tight-6, Gap-6, etc.

3. Attack the offense with individual stunts from the basic defenses used.

4. Attack the offense with individual stunts from other than the basic defense employed.

5. Attack the offense with team stunts from the basic defense or defenses.

6. Attack the offense with team stunts from a new defense or another defense utilized for that particular game.

7. The defense could attack the offense at different angles (slants and loops) with the basic defense used throughout the year.

8. However, the defensive coach with the utilization of a new defense could angle (slant and loop).

9. A coach could attack an offensive passing game with an entire new defensive pass coverage than used in the past. For example, if he uses primarily a zone defense, he could adjust and attack the passing game with man-to-man coverage and possibly do more stunting up front.

10. A coach could employ a new defense and an entirely new defensive secondary. For example, if the Wide-Tackle 6 Defense is used and the coach decides to use a 6-1 Defense with a four-deep secondary, more could be accomplished against a good passing game with an extra pass defender.

2

The Eight
Most Widely Used
Attacking Defenses

The defenses that will be explained and illustrated in detail are utilized to a great extent in football today. The defenses shown are the 4-4-3 Split Even-Diamond, the 4-3-4 Pro Even-Box and the 5-4-2 Oklahoma Odd-Box Defenses. Many coaches employ these defenses and may use different alignments, techniques and fundamentals, but the basic theories and concepts of each defense remain similar. For example, numerous coaches align the outside linebackers in the Split 4-4 Defense on the inside shoulder of the second inside receiver (usually the tight end or slotback). However, there are many others that align the linebacker head-up and attempt to accomplish the same job. It is the individual decision of the coach to execute the particular defense he desires and position his personnel in a way that will get the job done.

EXECUTING THE SPLIT-4 DEFENSE

The Split 4-4 Even-Diamond Defense is an eight-man defensive front with a three-deep diamond secondary. The defense basically consists of four defensive linemen (two ends and two tackles), four linebackers (two inside and two outside), and a three-deep pass defense. Diagrams 2-1a and 2-1b illustrate the alignments of the Split-4 Defense. As can be seen, the inside linebackers are aligned off the football in approximately the center-guard seams. The defensive tackles are on the line of scrimmage in the guard-tackle gap, while the outside linebackers are either aligned on the inside shoulder delivering a blow, or positioned in a head-up position. The defensive ends are stationed approximately 1½ yards from the outside linebackers on the line of scrimmage. Their stance can be a two-point facing into the ball, or in another position with their shoulders parallel to the line of scrimmage. The defensive ends can also be in a three-point stance, prepared to squeeze and contain the football.

The purpose of the defense is to get both a penetrating movement (by the defensive tackles and ends), hoping to put pressure on the offense, and a pursuing action from the defensive linebackers to help support the line. Another aspect of the defense is the ability to stunt with four linebackers and four linemen. The linebackers, however, must be mobile enough to help and support the defensive secondary versus different pass patterns and pass actions.

The following are the alignments, stances, initial movements and execution, responsibilities and coaching points of every position in the Split-4 Defense.

Defensive Inside Linebackers (Number 1 Men)

Alignment: The strong-side linebacker, or man to the formation, should align approximately 1 foot to 1 yard off the heels of the down defensive tackle, with the outside foot aligned directly behind the inside foot of the defensive tackle. The weakside linebacker away from the formation will be approximately the same depth, but will straddle the inside leg of the away defensive tackle.

Stance: A low, two-point, upright stance with the feet approximately parallel to each other. There should be no more than a toe-heel relationship.

Initial Movement and Execution: Read through the offensive guards to the quarterback, fullback and near halfback. Be alert for a play up the middle, such

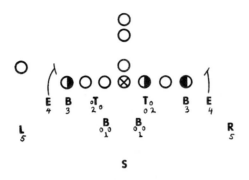

Diagram 2-1a

With this alignment, the defensive tackles are positioned upfield and the outside linebackers are aligned on the inside shoulder of the tight ends.

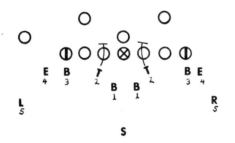

Diagram 2-1b

This alignment is different because the defensive tackles are pointed in, shooting over the offensive guard, and the outside linebackers are stationed in a head-up position.

as the quarterback sneak, wedge or trap. If the play comes up the middle, step quickly with the inside foot into the offensive guard. If the play goes to the outside, slide or shuffle the feet over the offensive tackle area. If the play goes away, the linebacker will step up into the offensive center and strike a blow with his inside shoulder and forearm into the neck of the center. The linebacker must protect this area for any traps, counters, bootlegs, etc.

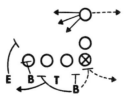

Responsibilities: 1. Play Toward — If an offensive back does not come or fill over the offensive center, then the linebacker will continue to slide along the line of scrimmage on an inside-out maneuver until he tackles the ball-carrier. If the play becomes a pass, the inside linebacker immediately goes to the onside hook area over the offensive end, approximately 10 yards in depth. He will attempt to read the pattern by the offensive receiver. (Some coaches will interchange the assignments of the inside linebacker and the outside linebacker. If the ball comes toward the inside linebacker, he will immediately fill over the offensive tackle area and put pressure either on the ball-carrier or the quarterback throwing the football. The outside linebacker will then support off-tackle, but will help in the pass coverage.)

2. Play Away — The linebacker first controls the center area, reacts to his keys and goes on a proper pursuit angle. On pass, he will rush the quarterback. (A few coaches will not have the inside linebacker plug as described, but will want pursuit along the line of scrimmage and assistance in the pass coverage with the defensive secondary.)

3. Drop Back — When the quarterback goes back to pass, the inside linebackers will immediately run to the onside hook areas getting a depth of at least 10 yards. They must read the patterns of the offensive receivers and attempt to pick up the receivers while they are in their zone.

Coaching Points: The inside linebackers must continually stay low and be tough along the line. Their shoulders should remain parallel to the line of scrimmage, keeping the head up and the feet moving quickly.

Defensive Tackles (Number 2 Men)

Alignment: The inside foot should align directly in front of the outside foot of the offensive guard. He will be approximately 1 to 3 feet off the ball according to the alignment of the offensive line.

Stance: The tackle will position in a four-point stance with the feet parallel to each other, head up and buttocks higher than the head. Shoulders are parallel to the line of scrimmage. (A few coaches will have the outside foot further advanced than the inside foot in order for the tackle to step first with the inside foot, because he is reading the offensive guard's movement).

Initial Movement and Execution: On the snap of the football, the offensive tackle will step up with his inside foot and attempt to go for penetration across the line of scrimmage. While moving, he is reading the blocking maneuvers of the offensive guard and tackle.

Responsibilities: 1. Play Toward — If the guard attempts to reach block (trying to cut off the tackle by getting to his outside leg), scoot to the outside; if he blocks away, close down; if the guard pulls, follow him down the line; if he sets for a pass, rush the passer; if he pulls toward, then follow the key and do not get blocked by the defensive tackle. In this instance, attempt to get across the line first and reach the outside. If this cannot be done, then take on the block of the offensive tackle and spin outside. Control the guard-tackle seam.

2. Play Away — Pursue the ball-carrier from behind and do not allow him to make a cut-back.

3. Drop Back — Rush the passer hard. One of the tackles must be responsible for the draw.

Coaching Points: Come across the line of scrimmage as quickly as possible. The more force that is initiated into the backfield, the more pressure is put on the ball-carrier. Stay low to the ground and move to the ball-carrier.

Defensive Outside Linebackers (Number 3 Men)

Alignment: The outside linebacker aligns on the inside eye of the offensive tight end, directly on the line of scrimmage. (A few coaches will use a head-up alignment.)

Stance: The linebacker will take a two-point, upright stance with the knees bent, buttocks down, shoulders parallel to the line of scrimmage and head up, looking directly at his key, the tight end.

Initial Movement and Execution: On the snap of the ball, the outside linebacker will step with his outside foot into the tight end and deliver a blow with the outside shoulder and forearm. Once this movement has been accomplished, he will look directly inside for any other blockers or ball-carrier.

Responsibilities: 1. Play Toward — The outside linebacker is responsible for the off-tackle hole. (As mentioned previously, some coaches want the inside linebacker to control this area and the outside linebacker to have only a supporting role.) The linebacker must be able to take on either a kick-out block by a near back or an offensive lineman, and tackle the ball-carrier. If the play goes outside, he will move from an inside-out maneuver not giving any ground. If an option develops, he will take the quarterback.

2. Play Away — The linebacker will cushion back into the pass coverage, not crossing an imaginary line on his original alignment. He will get depth of approximately 12-15 yards. If, however, the ball-carrier crosses the line of scrimmage, he will immediately go on pursuit. He must watch for any counters or bootlegs while he is cushioning.

3. Drop Back — The outside linebacker will automatically look for the curl area but think flat. If no receiver goes to the flat, then he remains in the curl area and attempts to read the pass patterns of the offensive receivers.

Coaching Points: When the play goes away, he must keep the face of his body to the direction of the run, and if the pass shows, he should break down in the hook area and read for pass patterns. If it is drop-back, however, he then turns away from the quarterback and attempts to read the pass routes.

Defensive Ends (Number 4 Men)

Alignment: Align directly on the line of scrimmage approximately 1½ yards from the offensive tight end.

Stance: Position in a two-point, upright stance. Shoulders are perpendicular to the line of scrimmage, with the end looking directly into the quarterback. Knees are bent and the body is in a good football position. (Some coaches want the shoulders parallel to the line, with the outside foot back. Other coaches desire a three-point stance, ready to squeeze down to the inside.)

Initial Movement and Execution: On the snap of the football, the defensive end will come across the line of scrimmage and get a depth of approximately 1½ yards. He will end up in a position with the inside foot forward and the outside foot back. This keeps the outside shoulder and arm free. He will key the movement of the first onside offensive back.

Responsibilities: 1. Play Toward — The defensive end must *contain* the ball-carrier to the inside. He cannot run out to the sideline to accomplish this, but must squeeze down any running room for the ball-carrier.

2. Play Away — Rush the play from behind, keeping a depth with the action of the football. He looks for counters, reverses and bootlegs.

3. Drop Back — Rush the passer from the outside-in. He puts pressure on the quarterback and attempts to read any screen if possible.

Coaching Points: Get across the line of scrimmage as quickly as possible. Take on any blocker by being low to the ground, and get the shoulder lower than his. Explode up hard on this man and hold your ground.

Defensive Halfbacks (Number 5 Men) (Only 3-Deep Zone will be covered. All other coverages will be explained throughout the book.)

Alignment: Line up 3-4 yards outside the offensive end and about 7-8 yards in depth. As the receiver gets wider, close down the lateral distance. After the receiver splits more than 7 yards, align on the inside shoulder approximately 1 yard and get 6 yards in depth.

Stance: Two-point stance with outside foot back.

Initial Movement and Execution: Key on your required man (offensive end?) On the snap of the ball, take one shuffle step back and read for run or pass.

Responsibilities: If the end blocks, react to the run. Approach the ball-carrier from an outside-in position. On plays away, look for the pass and then pursue. It is very important to be aware of the fake block and then a pass release. If the offensive end pass-blocks or releases downfield, play the pass first and then react to the run.

1. Play Toward — Deep outside one-third unless indicated otherwise.

2. Play Away — Deep outside one-third unless indicated otherwise.

3. Drop Back — Deep outside one-third unless indicated otherwise.

Coaching Points: Remain as deep as the deepest receiver. When the ball is thrown, go quickly and play the ball at its highest point. Play the receiver when he is in your zone. Attempt to read the pass patterns of the offensive receivers.

Defensive Safety

Alignment: Align over the offensive guard to either the strength of the formation or the widest part of the field. Be at a depth of approximately 12-13 yards. This will radically change due to widths of wide-outs, coverages, down and distance and score of the game.

Stance: Two-point stance facing the strength of the formation or field.

Initial Movement and Execution: Watch your required key. On the snap of the ball, shuffle back one step and read the offensive play.

Responsibilities: On any offensive play, the safety must think "pass" first and "run" second. The defensive safety will only help on runs when he definitely knows it is not a pass.

1. Play Toward — Deep middle one-third of field unless indicated otherwise.

2. Play Away — Deep middle one-third of field unless indicated otherwise.

3. Drop Back — Deep middle of field unless indicated otherwise.

Coaching Points: The defensive safety must attempt to know all the different pass patterns of the opponent and be able to read these as they occur. Play as deep as the deepest receiver. Sprint to the football and go through the receiver to get to the ball if necessary.

EXECUTING THE PRO 4-3 DEFENSE

There are many ways to execute a 4-3-4 Defense. Some coaches position the defensive linebackers over the offensive tackles approximately 1½ yards in depth. Another method to play the 4-3 is to align the outside linebackers in a stack position directly behind the defensive end. Other coaches will align the outside linebacker on the inside shoulder of the tight end and station the defensive end about 1 yard outside the end. These alignment procedures are shown in Diagrams 2-2a, 2-2b and 2-2c. However, the alignment and responsibilities of the Pro 4-3 are slightly different than what is indicated. While the defensive secondary coverages, middle linebackers and tackles can remain similar, the defensive end aligns on the outside shoulder of the defensive tackle, and the outside linebacker positions on the outside eye or head-up according to the split of the tight end. This is illustrated in Diagram 2-3. It is an even defense with no linemen aligned directly on the nose of the offensive center. It is basically a contain-and-pursue type of defense with a nine-man defensive front also. Since there are four secondary defenders, a great deal of pass coverages can be employed. Better underneath coverage is added when a defensive linebacker is aligned over the offensive end for pass defense. The defense is strong, also, because the defensive tackles are aligned over the offensive guards. The following is the play and execution of the Pro 4-3 Defense.

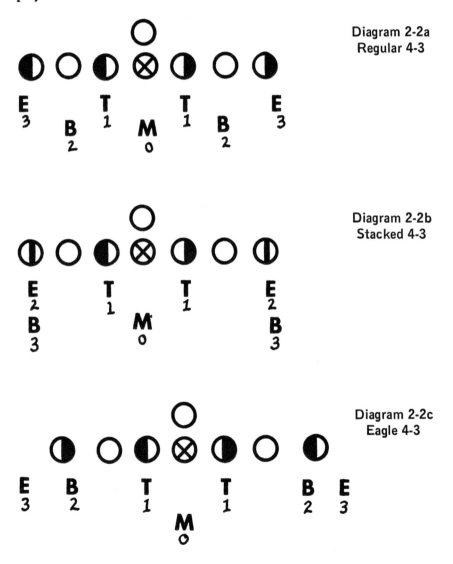

Diagram 2-2a
Regular 4-3

Diagram 2-2b
Stacked 4-3

Diagram 2-2c
Eagle 4-3

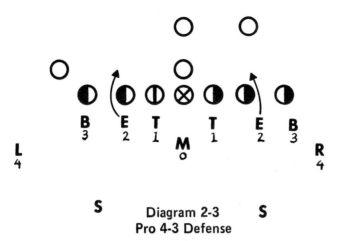

Diagram 2-3
Pro 4-3 Defense

Defensive Middle Linebacker (Number 0 Man)

Alignment: Line head-up on the offensive center with the feet at least 1 foot deeper than the heels of the defensive tackles.

Stance: Two-point stance in a good football position.

Initial Movement and Execution: Key through the quarterback into the backfield. Control over center area if run and be in position to make plays along the line of scrimmage.

Responsibilities: If the center blocks down either way, come up and fill. Watch for isolation and traps. If center fires out, fight pressure and go to the ball. You must not be hooked by the center.

1. Play Toward — Make any play straight at you and move from an inside-out direction.

2. Play Away — Pursue quickly.

3. Drop Back — Go to the required hook area. Watch for draw or any screen.

Coaching Points: Do not align tight to the offensive center. Attempt to read the patterns of the receivers on pass cuts.

Defensive Tackles (Number 1 Men)

Alignment: Align on the outside eye (or shoulder) of the offensive guard.

Stance: Three- or four-point defensive stance.

Initial Movement and Execution: Step with the inside foot, shoulder and forearm into the offensive guard. Key and read his block.

Responsibilities: If guard blocks down, move down and look for trap. Keep him off the middle linebacker. Do not be hooked by the guard. Follow guard down the line if he should pull.

1. Play Toward — Offensive guard area.

2. Play Away — Pursue; do not run around.

3. Drop Back — Rush the passer hard from the inside. Watch for the draw play.

Coaching Points: Look for any type of trap. Stay low with head up. Keep shoulders parallel to the line of scrimmage. If any definite passing situation arises, attempt to go for penetration.

Defensive End (Number 2 Men)

Alignment: Align loosely on the outside shoulder of the offensive tackle directly on the line of scrimmage.

Stance: Three-point stance with inside foot forward and shoulders parallel to the line of scrimmage.

Initial Movement and Execution: On the snap of the football, come directly across the line of scrimmage and gain depth of about 1 yard. Read through the tackle to the near back. Keep the outside arm and leg free.

Responsibilities: 1. Play Toward — If the offensive tackle blocks out, attempt to squeeze to the inside. Do not be hooked. If the tackle blocks down, look for the trap. If the tackle sets for pass, rush hard from the outside-in. The defensive end must contain on all passes. (This can be altered with the outside linebacker.)

2. Play Away — Chase the play and get as deep as the ball. Look for any counters, reverses or bootlegs.

3. Drop Back — Rush the passer from the outside-in.

Coaching Points: Stay low when coming across the line. Try to get penetration if double-teamed by the offensive tackle and end.

Defensive Outside Linebacker (Number 3 Men)

Alignment: Align head-up on the offensive end.

Stance: Two-point in a good football position.

Initial Movement and Execution: Deliver a blow with the inside shoulder and forearm into the neck of the end. Read the end block and look for the ball.

Responsibilities: 1. Play Toward — Offensive end area - Support on run. If pass, sprint to the curl area. If the sprint-out is hurting the defense, then rush the passer from the outside-in when the play comes toward. Can adjust to Eagle 4-3 if this should occur.

2. Play Away — Cushion back for pass, and once run develops, pursue to the ball-carrier.

3. Drop Back — Go directly to the curl area and read the receiver's patterns. Of course, this maneuver can change according to the defensive coverage called.

Coaching Points: Deliver a blow hard into the tight end. A hand shiver can be utilized. Try to hold ground versus a one-on-one block.

Cornerbacks (Number 4 Men) (Only the rotate coverage will be discussed at this point.)

Alignment: Three to 4 yards outside offensive tight end and approximately 4 yards off the line of scrimmage. This will alter due to splits of the receivers and adjustments to secondary coverages.

Stance: Two-point semi-upright position, with outside foot back, toes slanted in and weight equally distributed over balls of feet.

Initial Movement and Execution: Shuffle-step back on snap of football and read the designated key (usually through end to near back). Determine flow of football. On any run play toward, come to the line of scrimmage and meet the blocker with the inside leg forward and outside leg back. Force the play wide and deep. Do not open a gap between yourself and the outside linebacker. Keep on your feet and skate on outside plays. (Numerous defenses require the cornerback to squeeze everything to the inside.)

Responsibilities: 1. Play Toward — Outside area on run, with flat coverage on flow pass.

2. Play Away — Revolve through deep outside one-third and pursue.

3. Drop Back — Cover the proper zone designated by perimeter call.

Coaching Points: Be able to communicate with the defensive safeties on all coverages and calls made. With deep responsibilities, get as deep as the deepest receiver. If flat coverage, read the move of the second inside receiver first then scan to the outside man. If no man in flat, the corner could cushion back for added help in the deep secondary.

Defensive Safeties (Number 5 Men)

Alignment: Seven to 8 yards deep on outside shoulder of end on side of call and over tackle away from call.

Stance: Two-point with outside foot back.

Initial Movement and Execution: Shuffle back on snap of football and key through the end to the near back. Fulfill responsibility of perimeter call.

Responsibilities: 1. Play Toward — Force all plays from the outside-in. Cover deep outside one-third if flow toward (unless coverage indicates otherwise).

2. Play Away — Revolve to middle deep one-third.

3. Drop Back — Revolve to the designated one-third on call.

Coaching Points: The defensive safety must think pass first and run second. Attempt to read the patterns of the offensive receivers as rotation is being executed. Communicate with all secondary men.

EXECUTING THE 5-4 OKLAHOMA DEFENSE

The 5-4-2 Oklahoma Defense is a nine-man defensive front also. However, it is an odd look with a man stationed directly on the nose of the offensive center. The 5-4 is used extensively throughout the country by many coaches. While certain techniques may differ from area to area, the theories and principles of the defense are basically the same. The 5-4 is a pursuing and containing type of defense. Numerous coaches desire to slant and angle from the 5-4, and these movements will be explained at a later point. Certain personnel may dictate the different techniques the defense will employ. As an example, some coaches want a small, quick middle guard while other coaches like to have a big strong man at this position. Following is the basic play of the Oklahoma 5-4, with slight differences indicated.

Defensive Middle Guard (Number 0 Man)
Alignment: Align on the offensive center ½ to 1½ yards off the ball.

Stance: Four-point stance with head up and feet parallel.

Initial Movement and Execution: Utilize a hand shiver into the offensive center on the snap of the football. Key the center's head and look for the football.

Responsibilities: 1. Play Toward — Offensive center area.

2. Play Away — Pursue; do not run around (unless stunting).

3. Drop Back — Rush the passer but be alert for the draw.

Coaching Points: Be quick on the center's movement. Keep the legs back and free. Shoulders should remain parallel to the line of scrimmage. A forearm shiver can be used.

Defensive Linebackers (Number 1 Men)
Alignment: Align on the outside eye or outside shoulder of the offensive guard and station approximately 2 yards off the ball. If the middle guard aligns in the center-guard gap to take away any split, then stack behind him.

Stance: Two-point upright stance with feet parallel or toe-instep relationship. Inside foot is forward.

Initial Movement and Execution: Take a quick jab step into the offensive guard, read his block and then flow of football. If meeting guard, hit with the inside shoulder and forearm and keep the outside arm and leg free.

Responsibilities: 1. Play Toward — Offensive guard area, then pursue. Look for the play off-tackle then outside. Utilize an inside-out approach, keeping the shoulders parallel to the line of scrimmage. On any pass, go to the onside hook area and read patterns of the receivers.

2. Play Away — Slide down the line and look for any counters, reverses, etc. Get depth in pursuit — do not be cut off.

3. Drop Back — Sprint to the required hook area and read receivers. Look for any screen or draw.

Coaching Points: Do not be hooked by the offensive guard. Make sure defensive linemen have correct alignments. Adjust the depth according to down and distance. Be a leader on defense.

Defensive Tackles (Number 2 Men)

Alignment: Outside eye to outside shoulder of offensive tackle approximately 1 foot off the ball.

Stance: Three- or four-point stance with shoulders square to the line of scrimmage and feet parallel (or toe-heel relationship).

Initial Movement and Execution: Explode into tackle with inside forearm, keeping the outside leg and arm free. Key tackle's block and look for the football.

Responsibilities: If the offensive tackle goes down, then shadow him down. Keep the tackle off the linebacker. Watch for trap and isolation blocking. If tackle blocks out, fight pressure. If he attempts to hook, get outside.

1. Play Toward — Offensive tackle area, and if ball goes outside, move from an inside-out approach.

2. Play Away — Pursue; do not run around.

3. Drop Back — Rush passer.

Coaching Points: Move quick on tackle's block. Look for the ball immediately. Keep shoulders parallel to the line.

Defensive End (Number 3 Men)

Alignment: Outside eye or outside shoulder of offensive end directly on line of scrimmage.

Stance: Two-point upright stance with outside leg back; shoulders parallel to line and head up.

Initial Movement and Execution: On the snap of the football, deliver a hard blow into the neck of the tight end and look for the ball. Can utilize either a forearm lift or hand shiver.

Responsibilities: 1. Play Toward — Offensive end area. Do not be hooked. Must contain all plays.

2. Play Away — Chase the play and look for reverses, bootlegs, etc.

3. Drop Back — Utilize an outside rush. Look for the screen.

Coaching Points: Keep shoulders parallel to the line of scrimmage. Stay low to the ground and be aggressive. Keep good leverage on the football.

Defensive Cornerbacks and Safeties

Same coverage as the 4-3 Defense. Diagram 2-4 illustrates the 5-4 Oklahoma Defense.

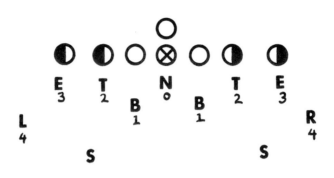

Diagram 2-4
The Oklahoma 5-4-2 Odd-Box Defense

STRENGTHS AND WEAKNESSES OF DEFENSES

When attacking offenses effectively, it is very important to know and understand the defense employed thoroughly. The theory and principles behind the defense, adjustment made, stunts and maneuvers utilized and secondary coverages employed are all very necessary to know when attacking an opponent's offense. It is a necessity to understand not only the strengths and weaknesses of the offensive opponent, but also those of the defense or defenses being executed. A coach can employ better and proper strategy to attack an opponent with this knowledge. The following, therefore, are the strengths and weaknesses of the Split-4, the Pro 4-3 and the Oklahoma 5-4 Defense.

The Split-4 Defense
Strengths:

1. Certain personnel make the defense strong.
2. The middle is strong, with two linebackers and two defensive tackles on an offensive center and two guards.
3. Strong off-tackle only if defensive linebacker on the outside is strong. If he is only playing a supporting role, then the inside linebacker must react fast in this area.
4. Strong on containment because of the placement of the defensive end.
5. The Split-4 is an excellent containing and pursuing defense with the placement of the defensive ends and four linebackers.
6. A great deal of stunting can be accomplished with the four linebackers and four defensive linemen.

7. Adjustments with the four linebackers to varied offensive sets can be done easily.

8. Can shift to other defenses easily.

9. A maximum rush can be put on the passer with stunting, and/or maximum defensive pass coverage can be employed with the four linebackers and three-deep secondary.

10. The defense employs a three-deep pass coverage.

Weaknesses:

1. The basic weakness of the defense is that it utilizes four linebackers to halt the running game.

2. Off-tackle can be considered weak.

3. Weaknesses can develop between the outside linebacker and defensive end.

4. The middle area can be weak unless the defense has the personnel, or adjusts the defense, to halt certain blocking and running patterns of the offense.

5. The flat areas of the defense are weak by alignment.

6. Motion may create weaknesses in the defense also.

7. The defense must utilize linebackers for a great deal of the coverages in the secondary. The defensive linebackers must be able to stop both the running and passing games of the offense.

The Pro 4-3 Defense

Strengths:

1. Certain personnel make the defense strong.

2. It is a nine-man front.

3. It is strong over the offensive guard area, with a defensive tackle positioned over him.

4. It is strong over the offensive tackle area because of the alignment of the defensive end.

5. The defensive outside linebacker is in a good position to hold up the receiver for passes.

6. The defense is generally stronger inside than outside.

7. The defense is great versus the drop-back passing attack. It is also good versus any pass with a four-deep secondary and the utilization of three linebackers.

8. The defense is strong in the flat areas.

9. The defense is strong in the hook areas.

10. A multiple of defensive coverages can be utilized.

11. A good middle linebacker can cover up and down the line of scrimmage.

12.   The defense can easily adjust to different offensive sets and formations.

13.   The defense can easily maneuver to other defensive looks.

Weaknesses:

1.   The center area can be weak.

2.   It is weak over the offensive end — Is the offensive tight end bigger and stronger than the outside linebackers?

3.   Is the offensive tackle bigger and stronger than the defensive end?

4.   The outside area at the corner is weak.

5.   The defense is generally weaker outside than inside.

6.   The Pro 4-3 is slightly weak off-tackle.

7.   The Pro 4-3 is generally weaker versus a running attack than a passing game.

The Oklahoma 5-4 Defense

Strengths:

1.   Certain personnel can make the defense strong.

2.   It is strong directly over the offensive center area.

3.   It is strong directly over the offensive tackle area.

4.   It is strong directly over the offensive end's area.

5.   It is a nine-man defensive front.

6.   A great number of defensive coverages can be utilized.

7.   It is an excellent containing and pursuing defense.

8.   The defensive linebackers are in good pursuing angles and positions.

9.   The short passing game is well-covered, with the hook and flat areas covered.

10.   The defense is good versus the Split-T attack.

11.   A great deal of stunting, angling and other maneuvers can easily be employed with the defense.

12.   The 5-4 Defense can easily jump and maneuver to other alignments.

Weaknesses:

1.   Certain personnel make the defense weak.

2.   It is weak directly over the offensive guard's area.

3.   Off-tackle is weak if certain blocking patterns are employed.

4.   Offensive line splits can hurt the defense.

5.   Outside the defensive end is weak for the running game.

OTHER DEFENSES TO BE UTILIZED

There are many other defenses that can be employed by the football coach when attacking offenses. The coach must continually be prepared to attack certain areas of the offense just on alignment alone. This can cause numerous problems for any offensive team. The following are a few defenses a coach could install, or may want to utilize, during the entire course of a season. The strengths and weaknesses of the defenses are indicated for the general knowledge of the coach also.

The 5-3-3 In Odd-Diamond Defense (Diagram 2-5)

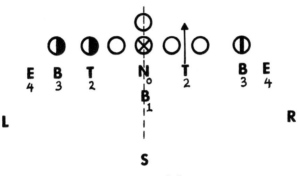

Diagram 2-5

Strengths:

1. Easily adjusts from the Split-4 Defense.

2. Stronger up the middle because of the nose-guard.

3. Adjustments from the defensive tackles can now be utilized.

Weaknesses:

1. Quick inside pursuit is not as good as was accomplished with the Split-4.

2. Some stunting is lost due to only three linebackers.

The Eagle-5 Odd-Box-Corner Defense (Diagram 2-6)

Strengths:

1. Can easily adjust from the 5-4 Defense.

2. Linebackers are in good position on the offensive tight end for pass coverage.

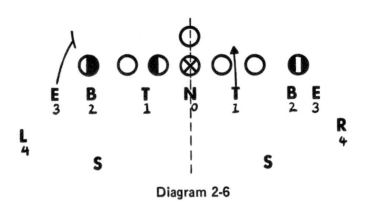

Diagram 2-6

3. Defensive tackles are stationed over offensive guards.

4. Strong versus the passing game.

Weaknesses:

1. Good linebacker flow is lost, as was the case with the 5-4 Defense.

2. Good blocking combinations can be used by the offensive linemen on the defensive tackle and linebacker.

3. Weak versus a good running opponent.

4. Weaker up the middle and off-tackle than outside.

The Wide-Tackle 6 Even-Diamond Defense (Diagram 2-7)

Strengths:

1. Stronger outside than inside.

2. Linebackers are in good position to go both outside and inside.

3. Strong off-tackle with the stationing of a defensive tackle.

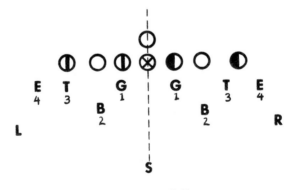

Diagram 2-7

Weaknesses:

1. The middle area is weak with three offensive linemen versus two defensive guards.

2. Weak over the offensive tackle area. Certain offensive blocking patterns can be employed.

3. Weaker in the pass defense with only two linebackers. The defensive ends must help out in pass situations.

The 6-5 Even-Box Goal Line Defense (Diagram 2-8)

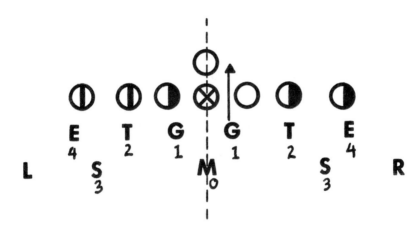

Diagram 2-8

Strengths:

1. Strong over the tackle and end areas.

2. Strong up the middle.

3. Excellent for pass coverage on the goal line.

4. Can easily slant and angle in all directions.

5. Can easily adjust to different sets, formations and motion.

Weaknesses:

1. The guard-tackle seam is considered weak.

2. Certain blocking patterns can cause problems.

3. If the middle linebacker can be moved out of position, the defense becomes weaker.

4. Weaker outside than inside.

The Gap-8 Even Goal Line Defense (Diagram 2-9)

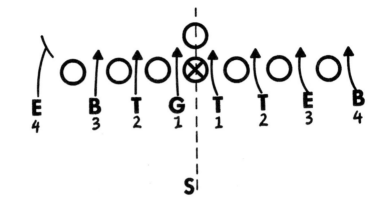

Diagram 2-9

Strengths:

1. Strong in every offensive gap. Stronger inside than outside.
2. Offensive splits are controlled by the defensive linemen.
3. It is an excellent penetrating defense, with good pressure put on both the running and passing games.
4. Excellent for short-yardage and goal line situations.

Weaknesses:

1. The center area can be trapped and considered weak with no middle linebacker.
2. The offensive linemen have excellent angles both for blocking down and reaching on the defensive linemen.
3. The defense is weaker outside than inside.
4. A great deal of pursuit is lost in the Gap-8.
5. It is generally weaker versus passing games and passing situations.
6. The defense has a difficult time adjusting versus varying formations, sets and motion.

Strengths and Weaknesses
of Offensive Sets,
Formations and Maneuvers

To attack an offense, it is important to know and understand the offense entirely. It is a necessity to know the formation it is being executed from. Also, once the coach realizes the strengths, weaknesses, sound and unsound points of formations, sets, offensive series, plays, and the different principles and theories behind the type of offense employed, the better he can take his defense and make the proper strategical adjustment and maneuver to attack that offense. The following are offensive formations with the strengths and weaknesses described. Offensive variations to these sets are indicated also.

CLASSIFICATION OF OFFENSIVE FORMATIONS

Offensive formations can generally be classified into three areas.

1. Closed Formations.
2. Balanced Formations.
3. Wide Formations.

Closed Formations

Diagram 3-1 illustrates a closed formation. This formation has everyone tight, and there are no split ends, flankers or wide slots. It includes a straight "T" backfield, three-back I, wishbone, possible one-wing back, etc. Following are the strengths and weaknesses of a closed formation.

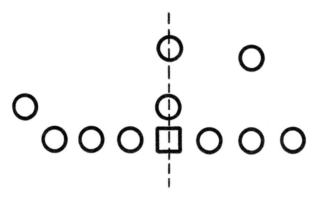

Diagram 3-1
A Closed Formation

Strengths

1. Strong inside.
2. Strong up the middle.
3. Good blocking off-tackle in both directions with tight ends.
4. Good pass protection on pass plays.
5. Can counter and trap easily.
6. A great deal of faking can be accomplished with three backs.
7. It is an excellent running formation.
8. Single wing blocking can easily be accomplished.
9. If winged, good for reverses, extra blocker, etc.

Weaknesses

1. Cannot run outside as easily, unless winged.
2. Does not spread and widen defense.
3. Must have inside attack go for formation to be effective.
4. It is not good for a passing attack.
5. Ends cannot release from the line of scrimmage easily.

Balanced Formations

Diagram 3-2 illustrates a balanced formation. This type of formation employs at least one wide man to either side. This could result in either a flanker, split end or wide slot. The opposite side is tight with a tight end, tight slot, wingback, etc. The following are the strengths and weaknesses of balanced formations.

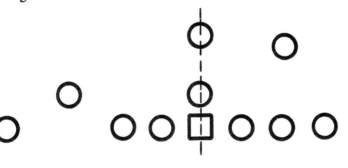

Diagram 3-2
A Balanced Formation

Strengths

1. There is a good, tight attack to one side.
2. There is a good, wide attack to the split side.
3. The formation spreads the defense to one side. It can get different defensive secondary coverages to this side.
4. It is both a good running and passing attack.
5. Split man can easily release from the line of scrimmage.
6. Can still get good counters, fakes and reverses inside and outside.
7. It has all the advantages of both the closed and wide offensive formations.

Weaknesses

1. It does not employ two tight ends for blocking. (If flanker, a good running back is eliminated.)
2. Does not give as good an over-all passing attack as in wide formations.

Wide Formations

Wide formations include wide receivers on either side of the center. This includes either two split ends, two flankers, one split end and one flanker and/or with a combination of slots. Diagram 3-3 illustrates an example of a wide formation with the strengths and weaknesses listed.

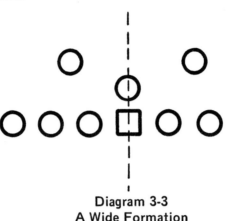

Diagram 3-3
A Wide Formation

Strengths

1.   Spreads the defense wide to both sides.

2.   Both receivers can release quickly off the line of scrimmage.

3.   Different defensive secondary coverages can be attacked.

4.   It is an excellent passing formation, utilizing both drop-back and sprint-outs to either side.

Weaknesses

1.   Not an effective running game.

2.   Not as effective running off-tackle to split end side.

3.   Not as good a running attack with two offensive backs. If three offensive running backs, there is no tight end.

4.   Not as effective (two backs) for fakes, counters and reverses.

VARIATIONS OF FORMATIONS

As previously mentioned, there are many variations of offensive formations. Every instance one offensive player adjusts to another position, it causes different adjustments by the defense. It is necessary to know these maneuvers so the defense can employ varied adjustments for a strategical gain against any offense. Formation variances can be divided into two categories.

1.   On-the-line adjustments.

2.   In-the-backfield adjustments.

The following variations are illustrated and discussed, with the advantages and possible disadvantages of each.

On-the-Line Adjustments

Tight End (Diagram 3-4)

□ O O ●

Diagram 3-4

a.   Good for blocking off-tackle.

b.   Can double-team with the offensive tackle.

c.   Can release for passes, but can be held up.

Nasty Tight End Split (Diagram 3-5)

Diagram 3-5

a.   Can still block off-tackle.

b.   Can double-team at the off-tackle hole also.

c.   Easier to release off the line of scrimmage for the passing game.

d.   Causes defensive adjustments. Widens men on the line of scrimmage or causes switching with the defensive personnel.

Split End (Diagram 3-6)

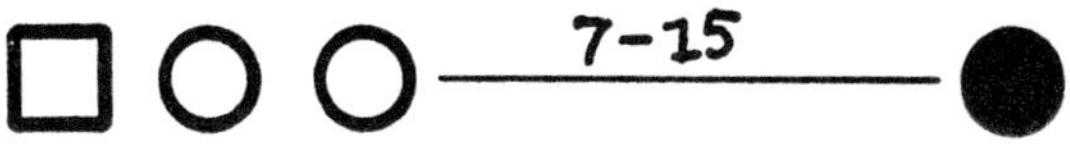

Diagram 3-6

a.   Gets a quick release off of the line of scrimmage.

b.   Causes the defense to spread and widen.

c.   Can come down to inside and angle block for wide plays.

d.   Difficult to block off-tackle, especially with double team.

Wing (Diagram 3-7)

Diagram 3-7

a.   A good extra blocker at the end, off-tackle and possibly over the guard area.

b.   An extra ball-carrier for counters and reverses, both inside and outside.

c.   Good motion man back to center area.

d.   Can get to flat quick, especially on the sprint-out pass.

Nasty Wing Split (Diagram 3-8)

Diagram 3-8

a.   Good blocker over the end area.

b.   Can release quicker on passes.

c.   May cause adjustments both on the defensive line and the secondary coverage. This may result in defensive problems.

Flanker (Diagram 3-9)

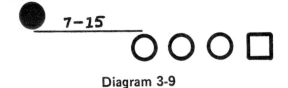

Diagram 3-9

a.   Spreads the defense.

b.   Gets quick release from the line of scrimmage.

c.   Can come down to inside and angle block for wide plays.

d.   However, it eliminates a runner in the backfield.

Slots (Tight Slot, Nasty Slot, Wide Slot) (Diagram 3-10)

a.   Same advantages as tight wing (tight slot), nasty wing (nasty slot) and flanker (wide slot), except defense is not always used to a slot formation.

b.   Offensive back is always in good position as a blocker, runner, pass receiver and motion man.

Diagram 3-10

Spread Slot (Diagram 3-11)

Diagram 3-11

a.   Two quick pass receivers to one side.

b.   Can release from the line of scrimmage quickly.

c.   The offensive back (slot) is eliminated as a runner in the backfield.

d.   Good blocking angles to the inside.

e.   Spreads the defense considerably.

Twins (Diagram 3-12)

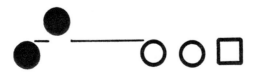

Diagram 3-12

a.   Same as spread slot.

Unbalanced Line (Diagram 3-13)

Diagram 3-13

a.   Causes defensive adjustments on the line of scrimmage and in the secondary. This may cause defense many problems.

b.   Good power to strong side.

c.   Can get to weak side quickly.

In-the-Backfield Adjustments

"T" Formation (Diagram 3-14)

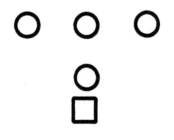

Diagram 3-14

a.   A balanced backfield. Can hit to the inside well.

b.   A great deal of ball handling and faking possible.

c.   Can hit quickly or utilize power to either side.

d.   Outside not as strong.

e.   Pass releasing not as effective.

Regular Backfield (Diagram 3-15)

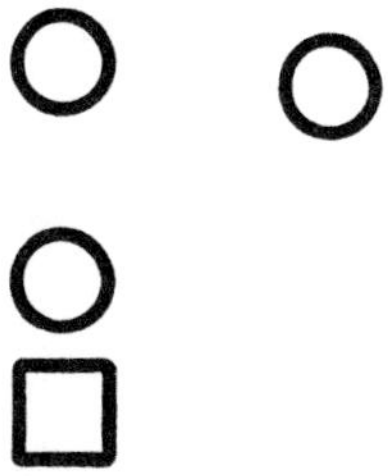

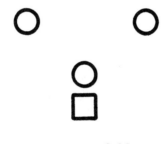

Diagram 3-15

a.   Can hit to one side as in "T".

b.   Good fullback threat.

c.   Only one back for a quick release on passes.

Split Backfield (Diagram 3-16)

Diagram 3-16

a.   Quick running to both sides without the use of a fullback.

b.   Two sides can release on pass routes instead of one as in regular backfield.

Backs Behind Guards (Diagram 3-17)

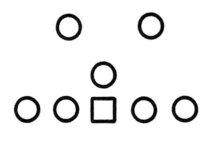

Diagram 3-17

a.   Not as quick to the outside as the split backfield.

b.   Good on triple option series, because of the alignment behind the guards.

"I" Formation (Diagram 3-18)

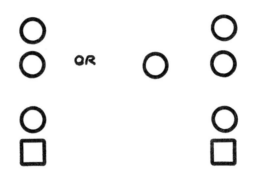

Diagram 3-18

a.   Strong up the middle.

b.   Best back in deep position can run to either side.

c.   If three-back I, more power and faking opportunities.

Wishbone (Diagram 3-19)

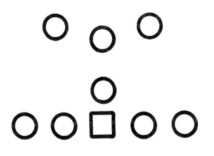

Diagram 3-19

a.   Strong up the middle area.

b.   Same as "T" except halfbacks behind guards.

c.   Good for the triple option series.

Strong Set (Diagram 3-20)

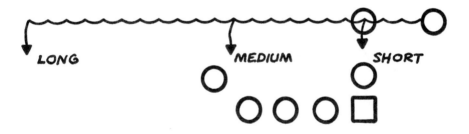

Diagram 3-20

a. Same as regular backfield except strength is toward formation.

b. Extra blocker to the running side (strength).

c. Extra receiver to strength of the formation.

d. Very little running or passing ability to the weakside attack.

Motion (Short, Medium or Long) (Diagram 3-21)

Diagram 3-21

a. Causes defense to adjust to its movement.

b. Puts the offensive back out quickly on the run. Good for releasing on pass route.

FORMATIONS WITH STRENGTHS, WEAKNESSES AND SERIES

The offensive formations that follow are some of the many sets that are seen throughout the country. Strengths and weaknesses are discussed with some of the play sequences that can be utilized successfully with each formation. While some series are not mentioned, numerous ones can still be employed.

The "T" Formation (Diagram 3-22)

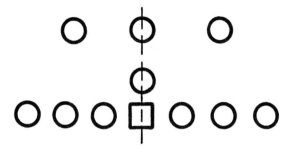

Diagram 3-22

Strengths

1.   Middle and inside strong.
2.   Counters, traps and faking available.
3.   Can get good power blocking with the three backs.
4.   With three backs, there is good protection for passes.
5.   Excellent for a goal line offense.
6.   Good for coming out of the critical zone (danger area).

Weaknesses

1.   Weak to the outside.
2.   Not especially good for a passing attack.
3.   Does not spread the defense for other possible exploitation.
4.   Cannot get good releases from the line of scrimmage for the passing game.

Series or Plays

1.   Split T if formation widens.
2.   Inside and outside belly.
3.   Isolation and traps up the middle.
4.   Power off-tackle.
5.   Cross-buck with halfback and fullback.
6.   Play action passes are good.
7.   Possible sprint-out pass.

The Wing "T" Formation (Diagram 3-23)

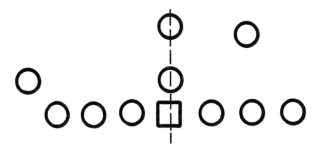

Diagram 3-23

Strengths

1. Same as "T" to weak side.
2. Wing is in good position for releasing on passes, blocking and counterplays.
3. Stronger outside for running.
4. Better for passing to wing side.

Weaknesses

1. Defense is not wide enough.
2. Less faking occurs in the backfield.
3. Dive man taken away.

Series or Plays

1. Inside and outside belly.
2. Power series.
3. Can sprint-out pass.
4. Split T to weak side.
5. Good for Delaware Wing T.

Double Wing "T" (Diagram 3-24)

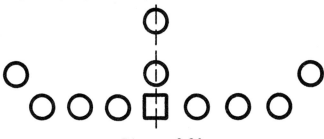

Diagram 3-24

Strengths

1.   Four men on quick release on pass.

2.   Can motion wing man back to halfback position. Defense cannot rotate one way or another.

3.   More of a passing formation.

Weaknesses

1.   Only one man in backfield for running.

2.   Not much faking in the backfield.

3.   Both dive men taken away.

4.   Not a well-balanced formation for running.

Series or Plays

1.   Must motion to get good series.

2.   Good for both sprint-out and drop-back passing attack.

Wing "T" — Split End (Diagram 3-25)

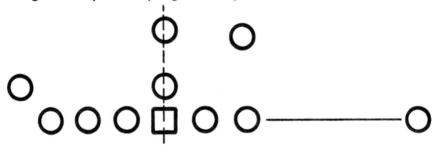

Diagram 3-25

Strengths

1.   Same strength to wing as Wing "T".

2.   Split end widens the defense.

3.   Better passing formation.

4.   End can release quicker from line of scrimmage.

5.   Split end has good outside-in angle block on the inside defensive people.

Weaknesses

1.   Eliminates tight end off-tackle play.

2.   Same weaknesses to wing as Wing "T".

Series or Plays

1. Inside and outside belly.
2. Good quick pitch series with the split end.
3. Sprint-out or drop-back pass.
4. Good Split T option to weak side with the utilization of the split end.

Tight Slot (Diagram 3-26)

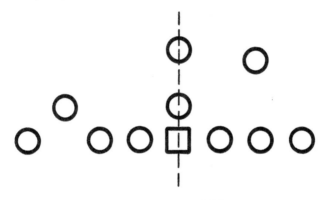

Diagram 3-26

Strengths

1. Same to weak side as "T" formation.
2. Same to slot as in Wing "T".
3. Since the tight end and back have switched, this may give defensive talent execution difficulties.
4. Tight end is in a quicker position to release from the line of scrimmage.
5. Slotback is in good position to block, run and release for passes within the offensive system.

Weaknesses

1. Same weaknesses to weak side as in Split T or straight T attack.
2. Same weaknesses to slot side as in Wing T attack.

Series or Plays

1. Same as Wing T.

Wide Slot — Split Backfield (Diagram 3-27)

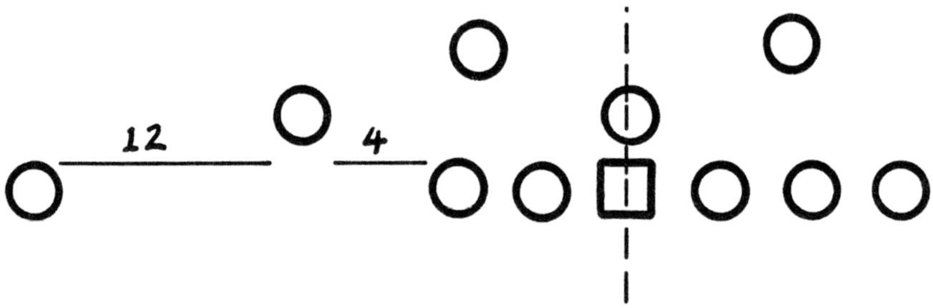

Diagram 3-27

Strengths

1.   Strong to slot side.

2.   Balanced enough to run to split side.

3.   Excellent passing formation (two quick receivers to one side).

4.   Two backs can release quickly on pass routes.

5.   Good power to weak side with the alignment of the tight end.

6.   Slot can both release quickly for the passing attack and still be utilized in the running game.

7.   The offensive formation spreads the defense well.

Weaknesses

1.   No fullback for quick middle plays.

Series or Plays

1.   Sweeps and power.

2.   Good for cross-buck series.

3.   Can quick-pitch to both sides; excellent to slot side.

4.   Good sprint-out and drop-back passing formation.

5.   Quick dive plays are good.

6.   Triple option can be run.

Pro Formation (Diagram 3-28)

Strengths

1.   Excellent passing formation.

2.   Two receivers can release quickly from the line of scrimmage on either side of the center.

3.   Widens and spreads defense considerably. The running game may execute better because of this.

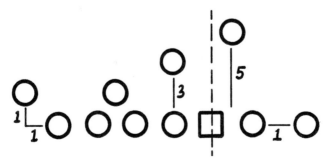

Diagram 3-28

4. Two offensive backs are in good position to release for passes also.

5. Well-balanced running formation to either side of the center.

6. Both wide men can angle block to the inside for the offensive running game.

Weaknesses

1. Only two offensive backs can run with the football.

2. Not as much faking in the backfield can occur because of this.

3. No fullback for an up-the-middle threat versus the defensive opponents.

Series or Plays

1. Excellent for drop-back passes (three, four or five men release).

2. Sweep series.

3. Cross-buck series.

4. Quick pitch series.

5. Quick dive plays.

6. Triple option series.

Single Wing (Diagram 3-29)

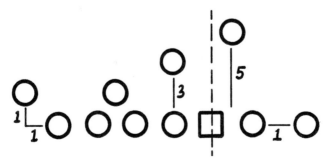

Diagram 3-29

Strengths

1. Makes the defense adjust to an unbalanced line.
2. Very strong to the wing side.
3. Powerful — two backs in position to block to one side.
4. Can get to the weak side quickly.
5. Good for passes with four men on the line to release quickly. Passer is all set and in good position to release the football.
6. Excellent kicking formation (quick kick).

Weaknesses

1. Not as deceptive as with a "T" quarterback formation.
2. Not as much power to weak side.
3. Offensive center must be accurate on the snap.
4. Protection is unbalanced for the passer.
5. Must have good tailback who can run, pass and kick.

Series or Plays

1. The spin series.
2. The power series.
3. The buck lateral series.
4. The drop-back pass series (quarterback or passer is all ready to pass the ball).
5. Reverses and counters are excellent versus over-shifted defense to strong side.

Double Wing (Diagram 3-30)

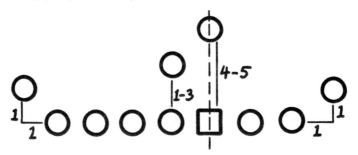

Diagram 3-30

Strengths

1. Unbalanced line may cause the defense problems.

2. Four quick men to release on passes.

3. More balanced formation than the single wing.

4. Two runners are in the backfield.

5. Passer is in excellent position to pass the ball.

6. Good for counters and reverses.

7. Good inside and outside running attack.

8. Good for the kicking game (quick kick).

Weaknesses

1. Not as powerful to the strong side as in the single wing formation.

2. Not as deceptive as the "T" formation.

3. Must have good tailback who can run, pass and kick the football.

4. Center must snap the ball with accuracy.

Series or Plays

1. Spin series.

2. Power series.

3. Good for reverses and counters.

4. Drop-back passes — passer all ready and in position.

Short Punt (Diagram 3-31)

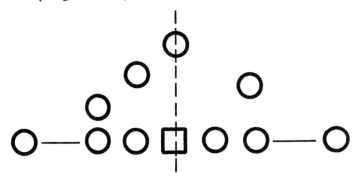

Diagram 3-31

Strengths

1. Strong to the inside.

2. Can get outside adequately.

3. It is a good balanced formation.

4. Three or four men can release on passes quickly.

5. Passer is in good position to throw the ball.

6.   A great deal of faking can be accomplished in the backfield.

7.   Good protection for the passer with good release for the receivers.

Weaknesses

1.   Not as strong to weak side.

2.   Center must snap the ball accurately.

3.   Tailback must be a good runner, passer and kicker.

4.   Not as deceptive as the "T" formations.

Series or Plays

1.   Spinner series.

2.   Power series.

3.   Drop-back series.

4.   Good for counterplays.

Shotgun Formation (Diagram 3-32).

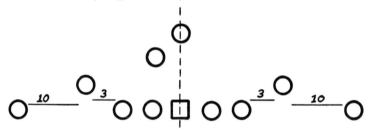

Diagram 3-32

Strengths

1.   The formation spreads and widens the defense considerably.

2.   Two quick receivers can release from the line of scrimmage quickly.

3.   Four possible receivers on passes.

4.   Excellent kicking formation.

Weaknesses

1.   Not as good protection for the passer.

2.   Not a good running formation.

3.   Must have a good passer.

Series or Plays

1.   Good drop-back pass series (quarterback all ready and in position).

2.   Possible reverses and counters can be used.

4

Attacking the Middle

The defensive coach must be prepared with his basic defenses to be able to attack any type of offensive play up the middle. The middle area of the offensive line (over the center and two guards) is not considered to be a dangerous area. Long touchdowns are usually not scored from this point because of the defensive team's relationship to the football. There are more defensive players who can converge to the ball-carrier resulting from the middle than can occur off-tackle or outside. However, if a team is not alert and fully prepared, a quick-hitting play up the middle developing from some type of offensive series can readily hurt a defensive team.

When attacking an offensive area in the middle, the football coach must have his players prepared for the following offensive maneuvers.

1. One-on-one straight blocking.
2. Cross or fold blocking (possible double fold).
3. Trap blocking (guards or tackles).
4. Offensive influence techniques versus the defense.

5.   False keys.

6.   Isolation blocking (one lead or double lead).

7.   Wedge blocking.

8.   Quick-hitting plays.

9.   Counters.

10. Inside reverses.

11. Offensive draw maneuvers.

ATTACK THE MIDDLE WITH OTHER ALIGNMENTS

Alignment alone may halt offensive plays in the middle area of the defense. Some of the alignments can be adjusted to easily from the Split-4, 5-4 and Pro 4-3 Defense. Others, however, may not be adjusted simply because of personnel and the type of alignments necessary to align in. The following, though, may offer the football coach some insights and ideas for attacking a team that is taking advantage of the middle area of the basic defense employed.

Diagram 4-1 illustrates a simple adjustment by the Split-4 Defense into another eight-man defensive front, the 5-3 Defense. Since the middle is being attacked hard by the offense, the defensive tackles do not have to adjust. Diagram 4-1a shows the defensive tackles either aligning or slanting down over the offensive guards. This type of defensive maneuver puts a four-on-three relationship in the middle almost forcing the offensive attack to go elsewhere.

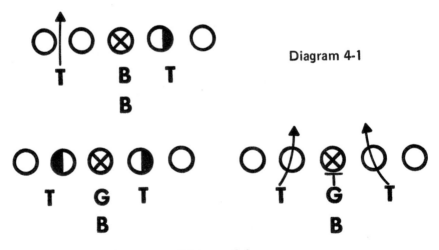

Diagram 4-1

Diagram 4-1a

Another adjustment from the Split-4 Defense is to jump the defensive tackle to the inside shoulder of the offensive tackle, position one of the inside linebackers over the offensive center and place the other linebacker in a 5-4 defensive look. This is illustrated in Diagram 4-2. A 5-4 Stack effect in the center-guard gap can be adjusted easily from either the Split-4, 5-4 or Pro 4-3 which is indicated in Diagram 4-3.

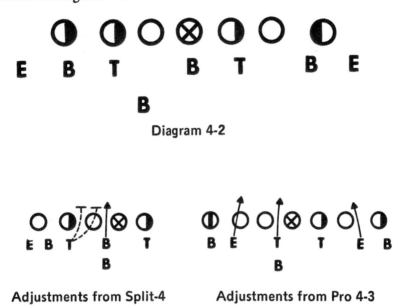

Diagram 4-2

Adjustments from Split-4   Adjustments from Pro 4-3

Diagram 4-3

A quick defensive tactic from either the 5-4 or Pro 4-3 Defense is to align the inside linebackers of the 5-4 (or the middle linebacker from the Pro 4-3) directly on the line of scrimmage. This is illustrated in Diagram 4-4.

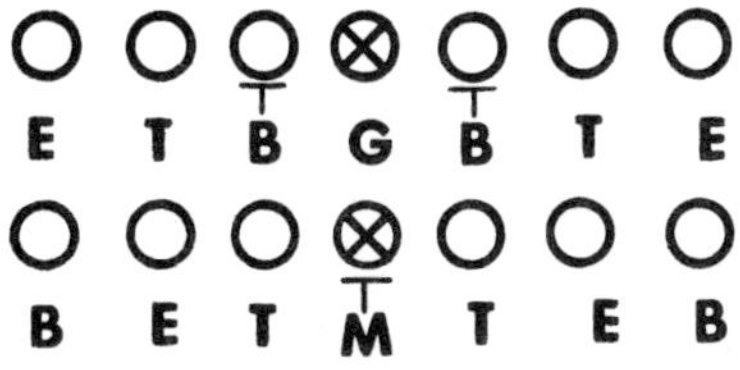

7-Man Look from a 5-4 Defense

7-Man Look from a Pro 4-3 Defense

Diagram 4-4

Another defense excellent for any middle attack, which can be adjusted easily from the nine-man defensive front, is the 6-5 Goal Line Defense. It produces quick pressure in the center-guard gaps, with an alignment of a middle linebacker for not only quick support over the middle, but anywhere along the line of scrimmage. This is indicated in Diagram 4-5. Other adjustments from defenses are illustrated in Diagram 4-6.

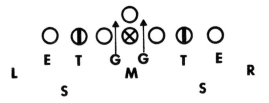

Diagram 4-5

From 4-3 Look

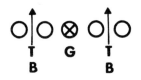

From 5-4 Look

From 4-4 Look
(4-4 Tandem)
Diagram 4-6

DEFENSING MIDDLE OFFENSIVE MANEUVERS

While alignments alone may take away certain offensive middle blocking schemes and plays, it is necessary for the basic defense to execute the proper techniques, fundamentals, keys and reads. The following are some methods, fundamentals and techniques to attack certain offensive strategies in the middle area of the defense.

Attacking the Trap

Defensing an offensive trap, especially by the players aligned over or around the offensive guards, can be difficult if they are not taught the correct fundamentals and techniques. If the defense does not require any penetration, the defensive player should *stay* on the line of scrimmage with his shoulders parallel to the line. This is vitally important. If stationed over an offensive guard, he can execute three different maneuvers of which two would be influence techniques. It is important that the defensive man be *drilled repeatedly* on all three offensive maneuvers. The offensive guard could block down on another defensive player. The defender must follow this man down as far as he can. If it was the defensive tackle from the Pro 4-3, he would attempt to strike a blow through the neck of the offensive guard, keeping his outside arm and leg free. As the guard blocks down, the defensive tackle would close fast and immediately look for the trap, unless, of course, he felt pressure from the outside. This could be a down block from the offensive tackle. If this does not occur, however, the tackle would take on the trapper (offensive guard or tackle) with his inside shoulder and forearm, shoulders parallel, head up, feet well-balanced behind him and look for the ball-carrier. The tackle should never put his shoulders perpendicular to the line as if he were utilizing a boxing technique. If penetration is not required from the defense called, then the tackle should never cross the line of scrimmage. This automatically opens a vertical hole in the defensive line.

Another offensive technique that can be used by an offensive guard (or tackle — whoever the offense wants to trap) is to "pull" in the opposite direction as if the play were going away. When the defensive man reads this, he should immediately *stay low*, take one step in the direction of the pull and look immediately to the inside for the ball-carrier and potential trapper. If he sees the ball-carrier going outside, then he can easily pursue. However, if he reads trap, he must close down inside and play the trapper, using similar techniques described previously. Another offensive technique used sparingly, but which is very effective, is to influence by utilizing a drop-back pass technique to get the defensive man to penetrate across the line of scrimmage so the trapper will have an easier block to execute. Again, the defensive man must attempt to read any trap from the inside once he sees this occurring. In most cases, both techniques of influencing usually succeed the first time when either is used by the offensive team. However, if the defensive man has been drilled to look for and read these offensive maneuvers, the defense can better attack the trap.

It is very important, however, that other defensive players assist in the middle against the trap. It is necessary for the men stationed over the trapper to close down inside, attempting to stay directly behind the offensive puller or trapper. If this can be done, there will not be any hole for the ball-carrier to run. Also, it is necessary that the middle linebacker from the 4-3 and the inside linebackers of the Split 4-4 step up hard into the hole, once trap has been read and the ball-carrier is coming up through it. Usually an offensive lineman will be sweeping across the middle area attempting to block the middle linebacker. However, if he can read and step up quickly into the line, the offensive lineman will not be able to block him. Diagram 4-7 illustrates the different maneuvers from the three basic defenses in attacking the trap block.

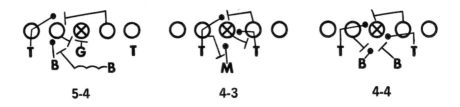

5-4   4-3   4-4

Diagram 4-7

Playing Against the Isolation

The isolation play is usually directed at a defensive linebacker somewhere inside the offensive end's position. It could be employed versus the inside linebacker of the Split-4, Wide-Tackle 6, 5-4, or the 4-3 or 6-1 middle linebacker. An isolation consists of one offensive back in the backfield exploding from his stance and attempting to block the linebacker on a one-on-one situation. Of course, there can be two offensive backs (double lead) used to block one linebacker. It is most important that the defensive linebacker key through his appropriate offensive linemen into the backfield. As an example, the inside linebacker of a 5-4 defense would key through the guard to the nearest offensive back. Since the isolation is going to be directed at him, the offensive guard will usually block down on the defensive middle guard. He could, however, block out on the defensive tackle. No matter what occurs, the linebacker, on this key of the guard and the movement of the nearest offensive back, must step up into the line, keeping low and in a good football position. He should deliver a blow by lowering his shoulder into the offensive back with his inside forearm and shoulder and attempt to hold his ground in the hole. The legs must stay back and under control. From this position, the linebacker must attempt to rid the blocker and make the tackle.

The other defensive players in the immediate vicinity must read and key their respective offensive linemen and pursue to the ball-carrier. It is very important when a defender is being double-teamed that he attempt to hold his ground and fight through the pressure rather than giving ground and meeting the ball-carrier. The isolation is a power type play run quickly up the middle, and the defensive linemen and/or linebackers cannot wait or give ground when it is aimed directly at them.

The double lead can be difficult to halt, especially if the defensive linebacker is not big or strong and cannot receive support from his counterparts. If two men come directly at the linebacker, he must again step up into the hole as hard as he can and try not to create any type of running area by giving ground. If this can be accomplished, the defense will have a better opportunity to stop the offensive play. Attacking the double-lead isolation can be accomplished sometimes on the offensive formation shown. For example, Diagram 4-8 illustrates a power I formation which has good potential for a double-lead play. Since the formation is strong to the left of the defense, the linebacker to the strength could easily maneuver closer to the line while the off-side linebacker could adjust back, giving him a better chance to get to the offensive play. Of course, the offense can direct a power or single lead away from the formation, but the linebacker who moved off the line has a better opportunity to take on one offensive back than he does two. Diagram 4-9 indicates the defensive maneuvers to halt the isolation play. Other methods to attack the isolation are to stunt hard into the areas being run at or quickly change the alignment of the defense.

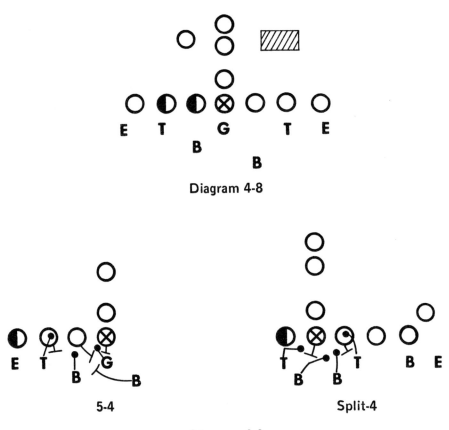

Diagram 4-8

5-4   Split-4

Diagram 4-9

There are instances throughout a season where a defensive lineman can be isolated, with an offensive back attempting to block him. If this should occur, the defensive lineman must be taught and drilled repeatedly to hold his ground, as was accomplished with the defensive linebacker, and go for the ball-carrier. This is not a difficult assignment, as long as he remains low to the ground and drives up through the offensive back.

Defensing the Fold Maneuver

The fold block is employed versus one defensive lineman and one defensive linebacker. Diagram 4-10 illustrates different folding blocks against defenses. As can be seen, one offensive lineman blocks down on a defensive lineman (can block out), and another offensive blocker steps around or "folds" on a defensive linebacker. Stopping this type of blocking maneuver can only be done if the defensive linebackers are keying and reading correctly through the blocks into the backfield. For example, if the middle linebacker in the Pro 4-3 reads the offensive center block-out on the defensive tackle, he must also notice the offensive guard coming around to make the block on him. This may be difficult, but should be practiced continually if the defense is going to stop the fold block and any play that develops from it.

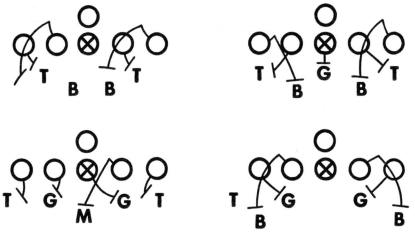

Diagram 4-10

Once the linebacker reads the step-around technique by the offensive linemen and the ball-carrier coming up through the hole, he must step up and meet the blocker as was accomplished versus the isolation. He should move quick and fast while keeping his body in a good football position. From this position, he will deliver a blow into the offensive lineman and look for the ball.

Defensing the Countergame

The offense, in numerous cases, will execute some form of offensive counter up the middle resulting from another well-established offensive play. At times, this type of play can be difficult to halt, especially if other offensive plays are running well and the defense is attempting to stop them. However, in order to attack this, the defensive linemen and linebackers stationed in the middle of the defense cannot react too quickly from their alignment until they locate the football and read if it is a counter or not.

Any type of counter usually has the offensive backs in the

backfield execute the play. The linebackers, especially, should key the backs and look for any crossing or counteraction occurring. If the offensive backs go all in one direction, a counter is usually not going to be employed. The defensive linebackers should attempt to stay on the inside shoulder of the ball-carrier which would include the action of the football. If a counter occurs, the linebacker has a good opportunity to reverse and come back for it. If, however, he pursues too quickly on backfield flow and the ball travels up the middle, the offensive counter will be a success, unless other defensive players are assisting. It is vitally necessary that the linebacker, while he takes an inside-out route, continually stay low, feet spread, head up and be able to either scrape up quickly for the ball or counter back to the ball-carrier with the techniques described.

Stopping the Inside Reverse

The inside reverse is an excellent play versus any quick-flowing defensive linebackers and linemen. This is somewhat different than the counter, because the ball-carrier is usually stationed either in a wing or tight slot position. In numerous cases, the defensive middle players do not see the ball-carrier coming from his position, because they are so intent on stopping the flow of the offensive backfield. If the inside reverse is finding success in the defensive middle, it is wise to adjust to another alignment, especially positioning players over the attacking area. This may mean altering the blocking scheme of the offense, which may greatly assist the defense. Jumping defenses quickly may be helpful. It is important, also, to try to slow down the pursuit of the defensive linebackers, especially if they are successful in stopping the other basic plays. Another method is to have the defenders key the wing or tight slot and give a "yell" when the offensive back goes toward the middle of the defense after the snap of the football. This must be drilled repeatedly if it is going to have any success in halting the inside reverse.

Attacking the Draw Play

Another play that can do damage to any good defense is the offensive draw play. It is usually necessary to make one defensive player responsible for the draw. When attacking the quarterback, this man should go for the passer, but be in a position to tackle the potential draw man also. This can be done by being aggressive but cautious, and always looking for the draw. If he is conscious of this, the defense will be successful versus the draw.

However, it is important to get other defensive personnel as supporting roles in stopping the draw also. Usually one linebacker can be responsible for this. He does not have to give up his responsibilities as a zone defensive cover man, because he will still sprint back to his area. However, as he is sprinting back, he should take a quick look at the possible draw area. This usually happens very quickly, and the linebacker may not be as deep as might be expected. If the draw does occur, he is in good position to stop his progress and recover to the ball-carrier.

Defensing Other Offensive Techniques

The one-on-one block is the easiest-taught offensive pattern of blocking. Yet, if the defensive players cannot stop this maneuver, they will have a difficult time in halting other blocking patterns. The defenders must be taught the fundamentals of stance, initial movement, execution, proper techniques (delivering a blow, keeping shoulders square and head up, pursuing properly, etc.), keying and reading, if the defense is going to be successful versus any offense.

The wedge block is another blocking pattern which at certain vital instances of a ball game must be stopped at the line of scrimmage. The defenders should "dig in" at this point and take on their offensive counterparts. It is the duty of the defensive coach to have his players prepared for the wedge-blocking scheme. It is necessary that the defensive linemen explode off the ball and meet the offensive line in the neutral area. The offense cannot come across the line of scrimmage, and the defense must get as tough as possible in not allowing them to do so. Getting across the line, keeping low so as not to lose any leverage and quickly looking for the ball-carrier are the responsibilities of the defensive linemen. The linebackers must be in quick support of the line and come up on the offensive ball-carrier as quickly as possible also.

ATTACKING THE MIDDLE WITH STUNTS

When the defense is getting hurt by certain offensive maneuvers such as traps, isolations, wedges or just one-on-one situations, the defense must quickly and strategically adjust to meet such threats. The stunt in the middle is a good maneuver to create pressure in that particular area. It must be remembered that with more stunting being employed, the defense should adjust to some form of man-to-man or half-secondary coverage (man-to-man and zone) in order to get good secondary pass coverage on the stunt. If zone is used, there will be certain areas open which are not beneficial for the defensive strategy or attack.

Using the Split-4

The Split 4-4 Defense is an excellent defense to put pressure up the middle because of the four-on-three relationship of the defensive front to the offensive linemen. Diagram 4-11 illustrates a simple defensive alignment from the Split-4. The defensive linebackers step into the line and automatically show a Gap-8 defensive look with the linebackers standing. Of course, quick pursuit to the outside and easier offensive blocking can result with such an alignment.

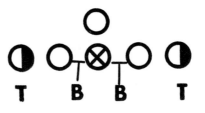

Diagram 4-11

The following are middle stunts from the Split-4 Defense (Diagrams 4-12 through 4-17).

1. Creates pressure over the offensive center without originally aligning in the position.

2. The linebacker should go through the neck of the center and look for the football.

3. The defense is really a 5-3 *after* the snap of the football.

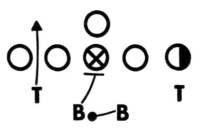

Diagram 4-12

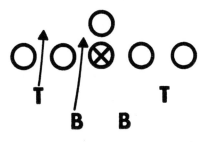

Diagram 4-13

1. This is a single middle stunt to either the right or left. Good for pressure on the side where the offense is running, or can be executed to formation or certain field position tendencies.

2. The stunt is excellent for pressure versus the running and passing games because of the movement through the gaps. Penetration is desired.

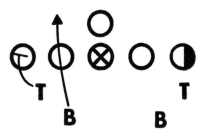

Diagram 4-14

1. This stunt is somewhat similar to the last defensive maneuver; however, the defenders are going through the neck of their respective counterparts.

2. While this does not give the pressure needed, as Diagram 4-13 illustrated, it does put pressure on the run and gives a better outside support to the running game while putting pressure up the middle.

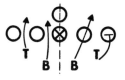

Diagram 4-15

1.   This is an excellent double lead up the middle. Pressure through the gaps or over the offensive linemen can be attained according to the strategic attack desired on the part of the defense.

2.   With the straight-ahead thrust on all the stunts shown, the defenders must remain low, under control and still key into the offensive backfield. Trapping can definitely hurt this type of stunting up the middle, and the defenders must be totally prepared for it.

Puts more pressure on run and pass.

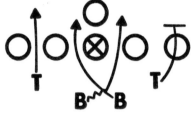

Gives good outside support.

Diagram 4-16

1.   This is a cross-charge between the defensive linebackers, and it attempts to use the advantages of the other stunts previously shown but desires to confuse the offensive blocking in the line.

Puts more pressure on run and pass.

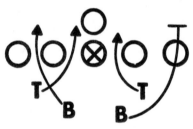

Gives good outside support.

Diagram 4-17

1.   This defensive stunt is the opposite of what was indicated previously. The defensive linebackers stunt outside and the defensive tackles shoot inside.

2.   The defense must, again, decide what it wants to accomplish and/or attack. The linebackers and linemen can shoot for the offensive gaps as indicated on the left side of the diagram. The defense can maneuver through the necks of the offensive linemen (shown on the right) in order to receive good outside leverage, and at the same instant put pressure up the middle area. Again, the defense must expect different traps, isolations, etc.

5-4 Oklahoma Attacking Stunts

While the Split-4 Defense had a four-on-three ratio, the 5-4 and

Pro 4-3 does not have this advantage. However, with the placement of the two linebackers and the middle guard in the 5-4, a great flexibility does exist for stunting up the middle. Again the stunters must constantly be aware of different traps, isolations, counters, etc. that can be used by the offensive team.

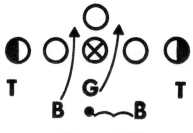

Diagram 4-18

1. This stunt puts good pressure directly in the middle with a "middle" linebacker free. The defense is stunting into a 6-5 Defense after the snap of the football.

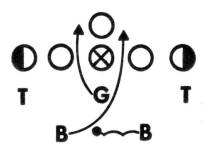

Diagram 4-19

1. This stunt attacks the same gaps as Diagram 4-18's stunt; however, the middle guard and linebacker switch assignments, hoping to confuse the offensive blocking.

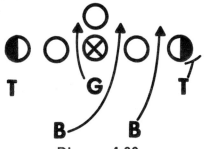

Diagram 4-20

1.   This stunt places a great deal of pressure through the offensive gaps, especially on the running and passing games.

2.   However, defensive pursuit is somewhat lost because of two linebackers stunting through the middle.

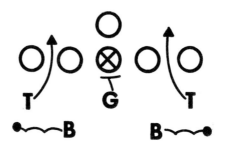

Diagram 4-21

1.   While this defensive maneuver does not put much emphasis on the passing game directly in the middle, it does give added pleasure to any type of middle action, such as isolation or trap blocking.

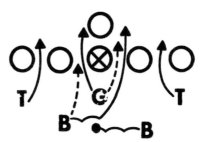

Diagram 4-22

1.   A great deal of pressure is obtained in the middle with this stunt.

2.   A middle linebacker is created to help support along the line of scrimmage also.

Attacking with the Pro 4-3 Stunts

The Pro 4-3 utilizes only one linebacker and stunting in the middle is somewhat curtailed; however, much can be accomplished to halt any offensive maneuver. Diagrams 4-23 through 4-25 illustrate a few of these tactics.

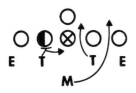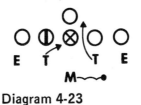

In this case,
the middle
linebacker
goes on flow.

Diagram 4-23

1. This stunt has the involvement of the middle linebacker. He can either stunt to the right or left.

2. When this stunt is called, the other defensive tackle should assist in covering the middle area over the offensive center.

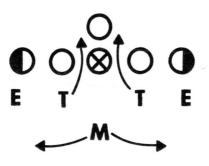

Diagram 4-24

1. This is an excellent defensive maneuver, because it places a great deal of pressure directly on the middle area and allows the middle linebacker to flow in either direction.

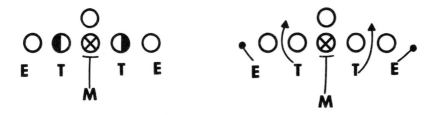

Diagram 4-25

1. The middle linebacker quickly goes through the neck of the offensive center and reacts to the football.

ANGLING (SLANT AND LOOP)

Angling the defensive line to gain an advantage is usually accomplished either to the formation, field or because of some other offensive tendency. However, the angle can be utilized not only for this, but to help support any offensive action in the middle of the defense also. For example, if the offense is running outside and off-tackle to the formation side and finding success with counter-plays and inside reverses going to the middle, a slant or loop technique by the defense for attack is good. The middle is being protected by a slant defender and all linebackers are free to assist anywhere (middle, off-tackle and outside). It must be remembered that stunts, used properly, can be employed with slanting and looping also. This would place more pressure on the running and passing game of the offense. Again, the defense will have to alter its defensive secondary coverage in order to attack any type of offensive passing game. The following (Diagrams 4-26 through 4-31) are some of the angles a defense could utilize up the middle area from the Split-4, 5-4 and Pro 4-3 Defense. If pressure is necessary to attack the offense, then the defense should utilize a slant technique to go up through the offensive gaps. However, if support is necessary without pressure, the defense can resort to the loop technique.

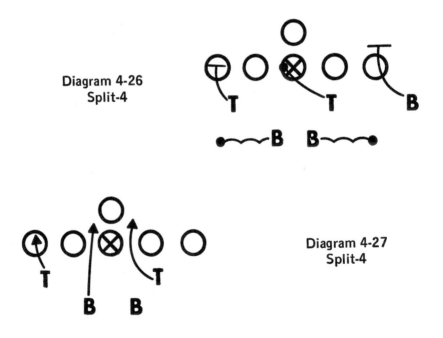

Diagram 4-26
Split-4

Diagram 4-27
Split-4

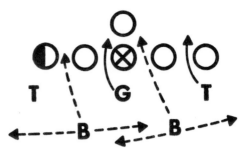

Diagram 4-28
5-4

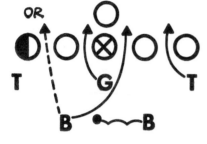

Diagram 4-29
5-4

Diagram 4-30
Pro 4-3

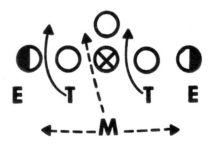

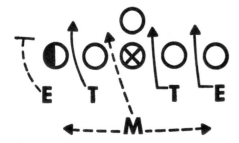

Diagram 4-31
Pro 4-3

Attacking Off-Tackle
and Outside

Numerous offensive coaches believe the off-tackle hole is the first area of attack when running against any defense. If they can establish any type of running game off-tackle, they surmise that they (the offense) will "control" the football game. The defensive coach, therefore, must be fully prepared to attack this offensive area as quickly as possible, especially if this is what the offense is attempting to accomplish. If the off-tackle hole is finding success, the offense can easily alternate plays up the middle and around the end. However, if the defense can halt the offense at the off-tackle position, the offense will have a difficult time attempting to run through the middle and then to the outside from that position. The off-tackle, therefore, is the critical area for any defensive team. Stop the offensive running game here and the defense can win the game.

There are a variety of offensive maneuvers that can be established off-tackle. Each one is designed to obtain as much yardage for the offense as possible. This is where the long touchdowns can begin to develop. The defense must pursue quicker to this area, and if any pursuit is cut off, the offense has the advantage. The defense must be prepared to attack the outside running lanes as well. The offense can strike at these areas easily, and the defense must be prepared for this attack also. When an offensive team goes to the outside, the defense must have good pursuit to halt any progress in this area. Of course, the defense must use its proper lanes and be prepared for any counters, reverses, bootlegs, etc.

The offense must be drilled every day on the different schemes of offensive maneuvers in each area. Once the season begins, the defense will only work in detail on the different blocking combinations and plays of the team they will face. If one offense utilizes power and brute strength, the defense must practice different double-team blocks with lead backs and linemen. However, if an offensive opponent utilizes more finesse, such as different option plays, counters, etc., the defensive players should be drilled in this particular scheme of movements also.

DIFFERENT OFFENSIVE MANEUVERS

When attacking off-tackle and outside versus the running game of an offensive team, the following are some of the actions the defense may encounter during a season.

Off-Tackle

1. One-on-One Blocking.
2. Cross Blocking.
3. Trap Blocking.
4. Double-Team Blocking (5-4, or 4-3 Defense).
5. Fold Blocking (4-4 Defense).
6. Power Blocking (Lead Backs or Linemen).
7. Kick-Out Blocking (Utilized by Offensive Backs).
   a. One or two backs can be used.
8. Down Blocking.
9. Out Blocking.
10. Countertraps.
11. Inside Reverses with Different Blocking Combinations.
12. Draws (Drop-Back or Sprint).
13. Double and Triple Options.

Outside

1. Double-Team Blocking.

2. Power Blocking.

3. Offensive Hooking Techniques (Used by Linemen or Backs).

4. Quick Pitch Maneuvers.

5. Outside Reverses and Bootlegs.

6. Double and Triple Option Looks.

The different offensive sequences or series of plays the defense will be confronted with are many. Some series are designed to attack off-tackle first, having different plays designed outside, and middle second. Other series strike outside and have plays run off-tackle and through the middle areas with different blocking combinations. Other series will attack the middle first, as has already been discussed, and have offensive plays designed to go elsewhere. The following are the different series a defensive team will encounter off-tackle and outside versus the offensive running game.

Offensive Series

1. *The Power Series* — Designed to go off-tackle first and run at other areas with different blocking combinations.

2. *The Outside Belly Series* — This series' main play attacks off-tackle first and will adjust to other plays later.

3. *I Tailback "Run-to-Daylight Series"* — Power is not involved. Usually run from an I set where the tailback is designed to go off-tackle, but will adjust his route anywhere along the line of scrimmage. Other plays are used to attack different areas.

4. *Green Bay Sweep Series* — Designed to run outside first, with other plays later going off-tackle and up the middle.

5. *Quick Pitch* — This series strikes outside, with other plays running at other areas.

6. *Sprint-Out* — This is included under the run to the outside, because some coaches want the quarterback to run first and pass second. Other running plays can easily attack other areas on the field, such as draws and counterplays.

7. *Option Series* — Different option plays are utilized to strike at the off-tackle position with an option or go outside to option a defensive man. Different variations include the triple option, swing option, etc.

8. *Other Series* — There are other series that usually run at the middle areas first, such as the inside belly, cross-buck traps, split-T series, etc. However, each has different plays from its sequence to run off-tackle and outside, with many variations and combinations of blocks and maneuvers.

ATTACKING OFF-TACKLE WITH OTHER ALIGNMENTS

It is necessary during the course of a football game when the offensive team has certain tendencies (game observations and/or scouting reports), to go off-tackle. The defense should be able to attack the off-tackle area with an alignment alone. If the defense is failing in this area, it must adjust fast in order to slow the offense down or halt it. This should be accomplished without weakening itself in other important areas of the field.

In order to attack the off-tackle position, the coach has a choice of the type of defense needed for any game situation. The following are four varied methods that can be successful in attacking the off-tackle position strategically.

1.   The defense must attack the off-tackle hole with at least two defensive people at the hole.

2.   Another method is to have two defensive players immediately at the desired location, but have some support (linebacker or linebackers) at the hole.

3.   The third scheme is to present a three-on-two relationship at the off-tackle position versus the offensive tackle and end.

4.   Lastly and probably the best formula to attack the off-tackle with alignments, is the utilization of three men at the off-tackle hole with some type of support (linebackers again) filling the area assisting the attack.

Following (Diagrams 5-1a through 5-1h) are adjustments that can be made from the 5-4, 4-3, Split-4 and other defenses that can attack off-tackle with alignment, employing the four methods described.

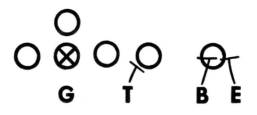

Diagram 5-1a
An Eagle-5 alignment adjusted from the 5-4. There are two men at the area of the off-tackle hole.

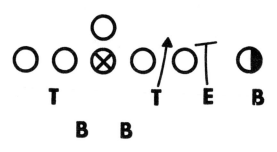

Diagram 5-1b
An Eagle adjustment from the Pro-4. Again there are two
men at the off-tackle area.

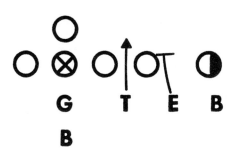

Diagram 5-1c
A Split-4 or Split-6 adjustment by bringing the defensive end
in over the offensive tackle. In this defense, there are two
men at the off-tackle position, but a quick linebacker for
support also.

Diagram 5-1d
This is a 5-3 or 7-1 defensive look, with the end aligning over
the offensive tackle. There are two men at the off-tackle
position, but a middle linebacker for support also. In this
defense, the middle is somewhat stronger with the placement
of the middle guard.

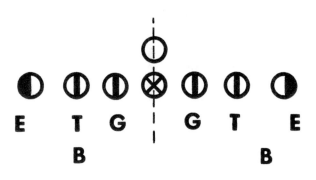

Diagram 5-1e

The 6-2 In Defense. Here there are three men at the off-tackle position versus the offensive tackle and end. The 6-2 Stack could be used also, as indicated on the left half of the diagram.

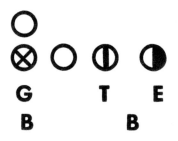

Diagram 5-1f

The 5-3 In Defense illustrates three men aligned off-tackle, but with linebacker support from the middle.

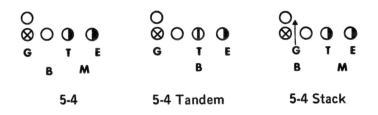

Diagram 5-1g

The 5-4 Defense and the 5-4 Stack is indicated with a rotated four deep, placing the "Monster" over the off-tackle position. Again, support from the linebacker helps the three defensive men. The 5-4 tandem is shown without any rotation.

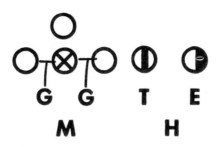

Diagram 5-1h
The 6-5 Goal Line Defense is a good example of three men attacking off-tackle by alignment, with support from the middle linebacker.

ATTACKING OUTSIDE WITH OTHER ALIGNMENTS

When attacking the outside with alignments, there are three basic maneuvers that can be accomplished.

1. The defense should have at least one man stationed outside the offensive tight end with some quick support from the outside. Inside linebacker support would be very helpful.

2. A second alignment can have two defensive men positioned nose-up to outside the offensive tight end. In this case, fast support should not be necessary as quickly from the outside. However, it is very helpful.

3. Lastly, and the best method for alignment attack, is to station two defensive players outside the nose of the offensive tight end. If there can be support from both outside and inside, even better.

The following diagrams (Diagrams 5-2a through 5-2f) illustrate these defensive concepts for halting any offensive maneuver that desires to attack outside.

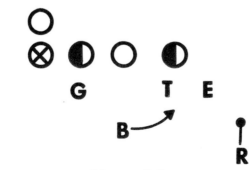

Diagram 5-2a
The Wide-Tackle 6 is an excellent example of one defensive

man (end) outside the offensive tight end, with quick support from an inside linebacker. A defensive halfback could rotate also. Other defenses could easily be the standard 5-4 and 6-1, with quick rotation from the outside. Each has similar linebacker support from the inside.

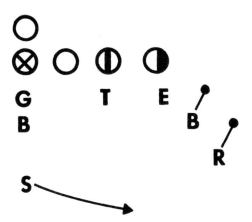

Diagram 5-2b

The 5-3 Out Defense indicates one player stationed outside, with quick linebacker support from the outside. A defensive halfback could rotate from this also. If the middle linebacker does not get tied up inside, he may be able to support outside.

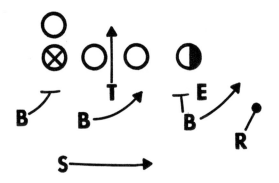

Diagram 5-2c

A 4-4 Tandem is illustrated because of the quick support of the outside linebacker both off-tackle and outside. Again, the defensive halfback could rotate for added assistance. The inside linebacker may help also.

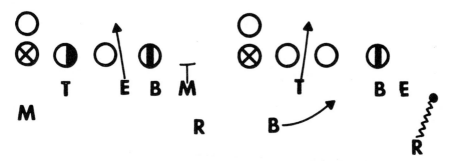

Diagram 5-2d

The second method is having two men nose-up to outside the offensive tight end. The left portion of the diagram illustrates a Pro-4 with a rotated Monster, and the right shows a Split-4 alignment. The same alignment could be used from a 5-3, Wide-Tackle 6 look, etc.

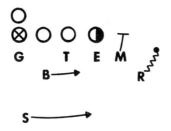

Diagram 5-2e

The third and best scheme to attack outside is to place two defensive players outside the nose of the offensive tight end, with added support being used from the inside and outside. This diagram illustrates the 5-4 Defense with the Monster on the line of scrimmage, with support shown.

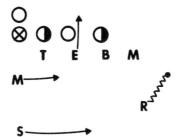

Diagram 5-2f

The Pro-4 with a rotated "Monster" is shown, with support indicated.

ATTACKING OFF-TACKLE VERSUS DIFFERENT OFFENSIVE MANEUVERS

As was mentioned previously, a defense should not attack at a position with alignment alone. Good fundamentals and techniques using the defenses installed should be executed also. The following are methods to attack off-tackle versus the many and different offensive variations and combinations of blocks.

Defensing the One-on-One Block

Any time there is a defensive man aligned either nose-up or outside shoulder on an offensive tackle or end, it is important that this man, on the snap of the ball, execute good techniques. He should strike a blow into his offensive counterpart, keeping his feet wide, back straight, head up, shoulders square to the line, body low to the ground and looking immediately to the football. When the ball comes directly at him, it is necessary to hold his ground versus the block, shed the man and make a good tackle. He cannot be pushed back, for this not only gives yardage for the offensive play, but also interferes with any pursuit from the inside. If a lead back or pulling lineman leads through the hole, the defensive man must again be low to take on this offensive man. He must step up into him and explode with his legs, back, shoulder and arm in order not to be driven off the line of scrimmage. If the defender can accomplish this, the hole is blocked and the ball-carrier will have to go elsewhere. Usually it is too late if the defense is pursuing to the ball quickly. If the defensive man can initiate a tackle after this maneuver, then he has done a fine job at the off-tackle position. Hopefully, some scraping or flowing linebackers will help support the play by quickly moving up into the hole to halt any type of offensive progression.

Defensing the Double-Team Block

The double-team block is one of the most important blocks at the off-tackle hole. This is usually true when there is a defensive man playing opposite an offensive tackle, such as in the 5-4 and the Pro 4-3 Defense. When this is the case, the defensive man must strike a convincing blow into the offensive tackle with his inside forearm and shoulder to keep his outside arm and leg free. While he is delivering a blow, he should be reading the movements of the blocking pattern. When he notices the offensive end or slotback block down on him, he must utilize his outside arm to help stop the force of the double-team block. His most important responsibility is not to be driven off the line of scrimmage. The defensive man must hold his ground if at all possible. If he does get driven off from the line, it is difficult for the defensive pursuers, especially the inside linebacker(s), to get to the hole being run.

The defensive man must stay low to the ground, and if he finds he is being blocked back, he should drop to his knees and attempt to hold his ground. This, of course, is his last resort. There are basically two techniques the defensive man can use to combat the double-team effort. The first technique he should attempt is to break the seam between the two offensive blockers. Usually the two offensive blockers are attempting to drive and keep their hips together in order to close the seam between them. The defensive player can try to fight through this area. One method is to turn his shoulders (very quickly) to the ground, reach out with his outside arm, spring off his legs and feet and attempt to go for the heels of the offensive blockers. Once penetration has been accomplished, he should quickly square up his shoulders, gather up his feet and look for the ball-carrier. If he can break the seam of the double-team block, he not only can stop any movement off the line of scrimmage but also cause confusion in the offensive backfield. He may stop the leading offensive backs or pulling linemen any way he can (Diagram 5-3).

If the defensive player cannot split the seam, then his next alternative is to "spin" out. After the defender makes contact and finds he cannot split the two offensive blockers, then he can drop his outside shoulder to the ground, swing his arm out and thrust it over his body, quickly snap his head so that his shoulders and body will follow, drop his buttocks to the ground and make a complete 360-degree turn. The defensive player should arrive in a good football position and step up into the hole for the ball-carrier. This defensive technique is shown in Diagram 5-4.

Diagram 5-3
Breaking the Seam

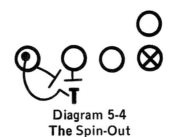

Diagram 5-4
The Spin-Out

Defensing the Cross Block

The cross block off-tackle can easily be performed versus the 5-4 and Pro 4-3 or any similar defense. Versus a 5-4 Defense, the outside defensive man or end must be the defender to break up this blocking pattern, hoping he receives assistance from the defensive tackle and inside linebacker. Usually, the offensive end blocks down on the defensive tackle; when the defensive end keys and reads this block, he should immediately step down to the inside and read anything coming from the direction. As he reads the offensive tackle stepping out to block him, he must lower his shoulders, keep them square to the line of scrimmage and strike a blow with his inside shoulder and forearm. He *must not* make any penetration across the line of scrimmage. By utilizing all of these techniques, the defensive end would naturally close the hole off to the inside. By keeping his outside arm and leg free, he is able to step out and reach for the ball-carrier if he decides to cut in that direction. Of course, the defensive end has plenty of support and assistance inside.

The defensive tackle should be keying this blocking pattern also. As he reads the down block of the offensive end and the step of the defensive tackle to the outside, he should react in that direction to help support the defensive end. Closing the hole by staying low and keeping the head up provides the defensive players with an excellent opportunity to halt the play.

Defensing the Kick-Out Block

This block is performed by offensive back(s) positioned somewhere in the backfield. It is usually employed at the defensive end (5-4 and Split-4) or outside the defensive linebacker position (Pro 4-3 or Split-4 Defense). In some cases, a double-team block can be used with two offensive backs.

Diagram 5-5 illustrates the kick-out block. If it is being executed by one offensive back, it is not difficult to combat.

However, two offensive backs can present a problem to the defensive player who is being blocked out. The defender must make his move and read the blocking combination that develops. As he notices the offensive backs driving at him, he should attempt to "read" the course or angle of the attempted block. This should be recorded in scouting and film evaluation also. In many cases, an offensive back will alter his course in order to kick out or hook a defensive player. If this can be read, the defensive end has a better opportunity to stop the play.

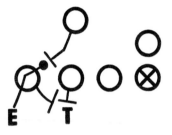

Diagram 5-5
Step at the Blocker to Neutralize Him

Once the defensive end has executed his initial step and movements and can see he is going to be blocked out, it is very important that he utilize good techniques. He should stay low to the ground with a good, wide base, knees bent, shoulders square to the line of scrimmage, head up, neck bulled and be prepared to take on any opponent aggressively. It is important that he does not penetrate too deep, because he will open up a wide vertical hole. As the blocker approaches the defensive end, he should step hard, explode with his legs, hips, back shoulders and forearm and meet the blocker below his shoulders. As explosion and contact is executed, he should squeeze the blocker back into the hole, shed him fast and look for the ball-carrier. In all cases, his outside leg and arm should be free, so if the ball-carrier decides to cut outside, he is ready to attack him. His shoulders must be square to the line of scrimmage so that he may get outside quickly.

If two offensive backs drive at him, it is necessary for the defensive end to stay low and attack the two blockers quickly, hoping to cause the offensive ball-carrier to go to the hole or cut somewhere along the line. Usually the defense can be prepared for such a block, because three offensive backs must be stationed in the backfield behind the quarterback to get two blockers on one defensive lineman as quickly as possible. Aggressive pursuit to this type of play is vitally necessary if the play is to be halted. Usually penetration at the hole and pursuit by the other defenders can prove successful. Waiting on the line of scrimmage and taking on power, can, at times, prove difficult to stop.

Defensing the Fold Block

The fold or step-around maneuver, as illustrated in Diagram 5-6, is usually utilized by the offensive team where there is a defensive player aligned in the guard-tackle seam. It can be used when there is a defender stationed over the offensive guard as well. When defensing the fold block, it is very important that the defensive tackle (such as in the Split-4 Defense) read and key the down block of the offensive tackle and be able to adjust his steps and techniques to get outside. This can be accomplished in numerous ways. Penetration can be initiated first with the attempt to maneuver outside. However, this may prove too late for support. The defensive tackle, therefore, while on his charge, should key and read the blocking combination of the offensive guard and tackle. When such a block is executed, the defensive tackle can step with his inside foot and react out into the offensive tackle's block. The inside linebacker should be reading the pull-around maneuver of the offensive guard and quickly get outside. It is necessary for the inside linebacker to strike a blow with his inside shoulder and arm so he can leave the outside arm and leg free. By accomplishing this, he can attack the off-tackle, and eventually the outside, much quicker. Reading, keying and reacting are probably the most important techniques versus a fold maneuver, and drilling of these offensive blocking schemes must get done every day.

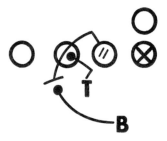

Diagram 5-6

Stopping the Trap

As was described in the previous chapter, it is necessary at the off-tackle hole for the defensive end or outside linebacker not to penetrate the neutral zone too deep. It is important to stay low, keep the shoulders square to the line and step down into the trapper while keeping the outside leg and arm free also. All proper methods on taking on an offensive blocker should be executed.

Defensing the Power Game

Attack power with power. When an offense is sending one or two lead backs or is utilizing a pulling guard, etc., it is important to get to the hole with the quickest pursuit available. It may be necessary for a defensive player to sacrifice himself versus the offensive onrush in order for the other defensive ball players to make the tackle on the ball-carrier also. The defense should employ intelligent and strategical stunts over the off-tackle area in order to get penetration without jeopardizing any pass coverage or other areas of the defensive front alignment. A great deal of pressure is added when stunting penetration is made off-tackle. The coach must analyze the off-tackle situation and react to the power with the best strategy he has in his defenses.

Playing the Counter and Inside Reverse Game

Usually any inside reverse or "counter off-tackle" is utilized when the defense is attempting to halt other areas of the offensive team and the offense catches the defense off-stride. The defense must be prepared to stay alert at all times for such a play to occur. If it has not already been executed by the offense at some time during the course of a game, it is of necessity for the coach to stress the importance of continually watching for it. The offense will be running some type of counter, countertrap, inside reverse, etc., in order to catch the defense by surprise. The defense must react quickly to the play, but perform their proper pursuit lanes, so they can react back to the counter. Playing and executing the defense properly is of utmost importance. Stunting or attempting to trick the offense, because it is being hurt by counters and inside reverses, may not always be helpful. The types of blocks used (usually traps) versus the defense, can be executed successfully on penetration movements.

The option game is very important for most offenses at the off-tackle hole, and outside also. See Chapters 9 and 10 for the complete breakdown of the option game and how the defense can attack it.

ATTACKING OUTSIDE VERSUS DIFFERENT OFFENSIVE MANEUVERS

Similar techniques must be used to combat the offensive maneuvers outside. The defensive players should be prepared for double-team blocking, especially versus the number-three (3) defensive man. This would be the defensive end in the 5-4 or 6-1, or the outside linebackers of the Pro-4 or the Split-4 Defense. The outside will have to face such tactics as power maneuvers, options, outside reverses, bootlegs, waggles, etc. While attacking some of these offensive movements has already been explained thus far, the following are a few techniques which have not been discussed.

Defensing the Hook Block

It is usually the defensive end who will be hooked by an offensive halfback or fullback. Again, the route taken by this back may determine whether it will be a hook or kick-out type of block. The defensive end should execute his initial steps and movements and read the blocking pattern and play being executed. As he "feels" the back attempting to hook him inside, the end must not allow the back to get to his feet. At all times, the defensive end must keep his outside arm and leg free, and therefore should keep his outside leg back and away from any blocker. As the end is being hooked, he should fight to the outside by using his hands on the shoulders and helmet of the blocker (Diagram 5-6a). By keeping his shoulders square and driving the blocker into the ground (since the blocker must aim low to get at the outside leg), the end can push him down and away from him. Once he has avoided being hooked, the defensive end can move upfield in order to contain the offensive play.

Diagram 5-6a

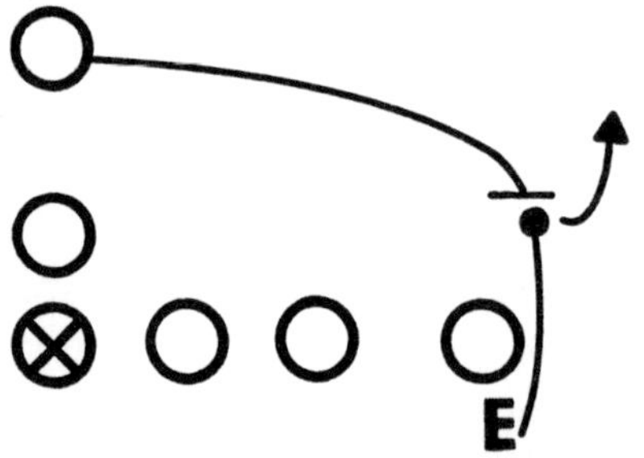

Defensing the Crackback Block

A crackback block will occur when there is a wider offensive man (usually a split end or flanker) than the defensive end or corner rotator, such as an invert defender. It is very important to be able to attack this situation. Basically, four maneuvers can be executed. The defensive players at the corner should align a defensive man either head-up or on either shoulder of the wide receiver. Position alone will help versus a crackback. If alignment is not desired wide, the defensive man positioned inside to receive the crackback can turn his back to the wide-out. Since the wide offensive man cannot clip in this area, he will have to alter his course or route to block another defender. The third technique utilized is to take on the block of the crackback with the outside shoulder, stay low and watch the play develop. Once the ball-carrier has committed, he can either penetrate across the line or pursue deeper to get outside. The last technique employed is to avoid the block completely by keeping an eye on the blocker, and at the last possible minute, move quickly either forward or backward. He should be prepared to initiate a tackle on the ball-carrier once the technique has been executed. At all times the defender must stay low, in a good football position, ready to react quickly and aggressively either way versus the crackback block.

Defensing the Bootleg

The bootleg is an excellent play for the offense, but can easily be defensed, especially the run, if the proper keys and maneuvers are utilized by the containing defensive men. The contain man (defensive end) must make his proper movements after the snap of the football. Usually on any bootleg offensive maneuver, the offense will pull one or both guards in the opposite direction of the play being faked. If the contain man reads this pull coming back toward him, he should stay low, keep his shoulders parallel to the line of scrimmage and take on the pulling guard with his inside shoulder and forearm, keeping his outside leg and arm free. His outside foot should be positioned back of the inside forward foot. Once this position has been made, there should be no difficulty in both squeezing and containing the ball-carrier (usually the quarterback). If he desires to cut outside, the contain man can easily protect this area because of his free outside arm and leg. If the quarterback goes inside, the delaying pursuit should assist and stop the play, especially if the defender containing closes the hole to the inside on his first read of the pulling guards.

Defensing the Quick Pitch

The quick pitch play develops so fast that the defense has only time to react as quickly as possible, hoping the defensive end or contain man can force the quick pitch ball-carrier inside. The defensive contain player must be drilled on this play repeatedly. The defensive men nearest the ball-carrier, after seeing the quick pitch develop, must scoot outside and attempt to penetrate across the line of scrimmage as quickly as possible. Gaining yardage into the offensive backfield and attempting to beat any pulling offensive linemen to lead the interference for the ball-carrier, will help a great deal in stopping this play. The defensive end must be quick and react fast to accomplish containment. Sheer power will not stop it, but quick reaction and pursuit will.

ATTACKING THE OFF-TACKLE WITH STUNTS

When the off-tackle hole is being penetrated by offensive thrusts, the defense must react quickly at this hole. If alignment alone does not succeed, the defense must go to a stunting game of some type. Secondary coverages with linebackers and halfbacks may have to adjust in order for this particular area to be sound versus any passing. The offensive option game must be halted also, and there are more individual techniques and skills used for this. Chapters 9 and 10 discuss these defensive techniques. Stunts and angles, therefore, versus the entire option game, will not be discussed in this chapter.

Stunting with the Split-4 Defense

It should be remembered that individual, group and team stunts can be utilized with any defense. The following stunts are only the ones utilized at the off-tackle hole when pressure is needed.

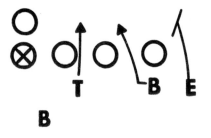

Diagram 5-7

Diagram 5-7 illustrates an outside linebacker and end stunt. The outside linebacker drives for the tackle-end seam, attempting to create pressure at this hole. He should not take an angle that will force him far to the inside. Rather, he should fight to go upstream so the offensive end cannot drive him away from the hole. The defensive end must come across the line of scrimmage, but squeeze hard inside also, so a gap will not develop between himself and the linebacker.

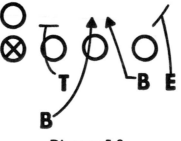

Diagram 5-8

Diagram 5-8 indicates the same stunt off-tackle, but with good added support from the inside linebacker as well. The same techniques are used as before, except the inside linebacker scrapes hard over the inside shoulder of the offensive tackle and tries to force penetration across the line of scrimmage. The defensive tackle loops across the offensive guard's face to an inside eye position on him. He must assist the opposite inside linebacker for any plays up the middle.

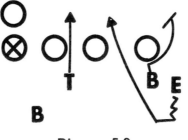

Diagram 5-9

Diagram 5-9 illustrates another stunt utilizing the defensive end. The end, before the snap of the ball, comes off the line of scrimmage and attacks the tackle-end gap, while the outside linebacker loops outside and contains the play. An inside linebacker scrape can also be added to this stunt off-tackle as shown in Diagram 5-10.

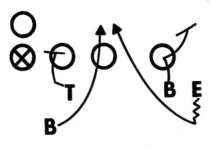

Diagram 5-10

Another excellent stunt is shown in Diagram 5-11. In this case, the defensive tackle loops outside the tackle-end seam while the outside linebacker steps behind and fires into the guard-tackle gap. The advantage of this stunt is it can totally confuse the blocking of the offensive linemen. The defensive tackle must cheat out slightly and beat the down block of the offensive tackle if it should occur. The linebacker must move quickly to get good position in the gap he is stunting.

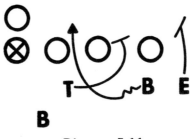

Diagram 5-11

Stunting Off-Tackle from the 5-4 Defense

An excellent stunt from the 5-4 Defense is illustrated in Diagrams 5-12 and 5-12a. Diagram 5-12 indicates a tackle-linebacker stunt. In Diagram 5-12a, the defensive tackle and end slant down to the inside gaps while the inside linebacker maneuvers outside. Diagram 5-13 shows the same method; however, the defensive tackle does not go hard inside, but rather loops into the inside shoulder of the offensive tackle. This defensive tactic will support the off-tackle hole more. Diagram 5-14 indicates another method. The defensive tackle slants quickly into the tackle-end seam while the inside linebacker stunts through the guard area. The defensive end strikes a blow into the offensive end and plays a normal 5-4 defensive end.

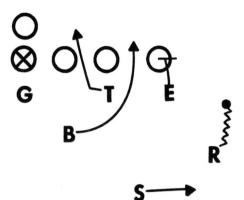

Diagram 5-12

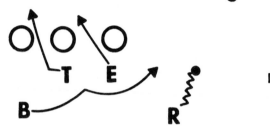

Diagram 5-12a

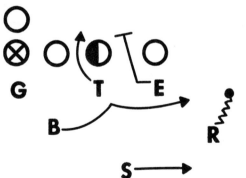

Diagram 5-13

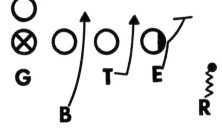

Diagram 5-14

A cross defensive charge between the defensive tackle and end is excellent. This defensive stunt can create havoc for the offensive linemen. At the same time, however, the inside linebacker is in good position to support the off-tackle area while the corner rotator can assist outside (Diagram 5-15).

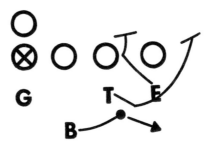

Diagram 5-15

A stunt which can cause a good deal of damage at the off-tackle position, especially in confusing the offensive blockers at the point of attack, is illustrated in Diagram 5-16. In this situation, the defensive tackle and end go inside and outside respectively, while the cornerback rotates up and stunts through the tackle-end seam. This places a lot of pressure on the off-tackle hole, because good support remains from the inside linebacker. The defensive tackle can either stunt hard to the inside or play the inside shoulder of the offensive tackle.

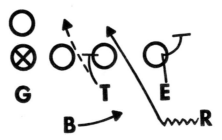

Diagram 5-16

ATTACKING OFF-TACKLE WITH THE PRO-4 DEFENSE

A few of the defensive stunts utilized from the 5-4 Defense can be incorporated at the off-tackle position with the Pro-4 Defense since the defensive look is similar in this area. A cross charge between the defensive end and outside linebacker can be made. A corner stunt off-tackle can be utilized also. Diagram 5-17 indicates an out maneuver by the defensive end. This can be accomplished by itself, or other defensive linemen can become involved, such as the defensive tackle and/or linebacker (Diagram 5-18). All of these stunts can create a good deal of pressure at the hole. When one, two or three stunts are initiated outside, the defensive middle linebacker must compensate for the areas that are uncovered because of the movement. The middle linebacker could either stunt in the unattended area or cover it and then slide to the ball-carrier. Diagram 5-19 indicates an "in" charge, with the outside linebacker putting pressure off-tackle. The defensive end could either go through the head of the offensive tackle, as shown, or stunt into the guard-tackle gap. Of course, there is more of a defensive attack off-tackle if the defensive end plays through the head of his offensive counterpart.

Diagram 5-17

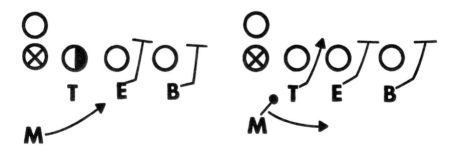

Diagram 5-18

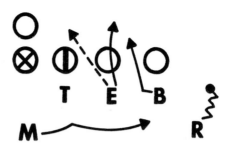

Diagram 5-19

ATTACKING OUTSIDE WITH THE SPLIT-4, 5-4 AND PRO-4 DEFENSES

Many of the stunts that were executed for the off-tackle hole can be used to attack outside as well. If the offensive linemen have not been drilled on the stunting game, it can create havoc up front against their blocking pattern. This will probably cause a breakdown in assignments. The following are a few stunts which can be utilized versus the outside running game (Diagrams 5-20 through 5-22).

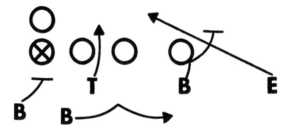

Diagram 5-20
A Split-4 stunt with the defensive end stunting hard to the inside while the outside linebacker delivers a blow into the offensive end and loops outside.

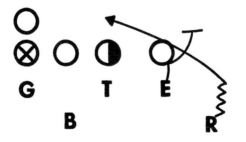

Diagram 5-21

A 5-4 stunt similar to Diagram 5-20, except the cornerback

rotates up from a four deep and stunts hard inside. The defensive end loops outside. The three-deep secondary can now rotate if necessary.

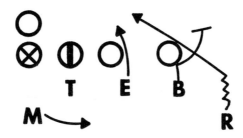

Diagram 5-22
A Pro-4 stunt is shown similar to the 5-4 corner stunt.

ATTACKING OFF-TACKLE AND OUTSIDE WITH ANGLING LINES

Slanting and looping lines can be very helpful in attacking the off-tackle and outside areas versus any offense. Secondary coverages can remain intact because linebacker stunts do not have to be executed. Diagrams 5-23 through 5-28 illustrate angling lines from the Split-4, the 5-4, and the Pro-4 Defense. Numerous variations can be used by each defense for particular situations. This would include having only half or three-quarters of the front linemen angle. Different stunts can be added outside and off-tackle with the angles, to create different defensive looks. Of course, different secondary coverages should be used if the defense is to remain sound in the numerous different situations that will occur in the ball game.

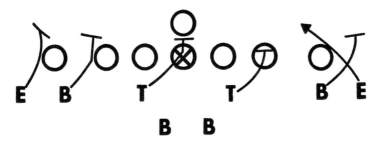

Diagram 5-23
An outside stunt is used in this situation. The angle is usually to the formation, field or hole being used most often by the offense.

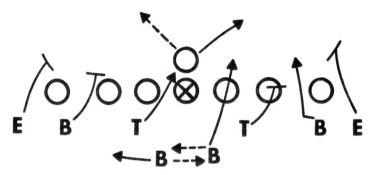

Diagram 5-24

A similar angle to Diagram 5-23, except the pressure is more inside or off-tackle. Notice the inside linebacker stunts to flow. This and other maneuvers can be interchanged according to what the offense is trying to accomplish.

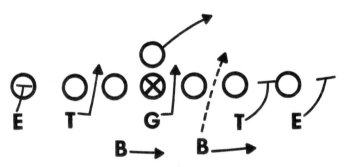

Diagram 5-25

The Angle Defense from the 5-4. A corner stunt could be used with this move, and many other inside stunts could be utilized.

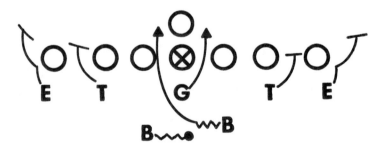

Diagram 5-26

An Angle-Out Defense from the 5-4 to both sides. Of course inside stunts should be used with this.

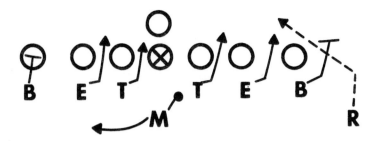

Diagram 5-27
An angle to the off-tackle and outside threat with the Pro-4
Defense. A corner stunt is indicated.

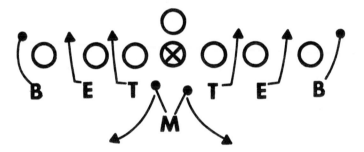

Diagram 5-28
An Angle-Out Defense from the Pro-4 Defense.

Attacking Wide-Outs
and Flats

UTILIZING A THREE- OR FOUR-DEEP SECONDARY

It should be readily understood that a team has a better opportunity to halt a passing attack or detailed passing situation utilizing a four deep rather than a three-deep secondary. The reasons are obvious. An offense can release, usually at the most (not counting the quarterback), five (5) individual receivers into a route or pattern. A four deep can cover five with the utilization of a linebacker; whereas, a three-deep coverage must use two linebackers. It is, therefore, necessary to find two linebackers who are not only strong and aggressive versus the running game, but who are also quick and agile, to cover certain offensive receivers. This type of defender is relatively hard to locate in a squad, and therefore it would be difficult to have your linebackers execute well versus a good passing team. The Split-4 uses a three deep; whereas, the 5-4 and Pro-4 utilize a four-deep secondary.

A coach must decide what type of defense he wants to install; i.e., a three-deep or four-deep principle. Most coaches in the country do not use a three deep and four deep combined with their coverages, because of the difficulty of executing both coverages and eliminating mistakes. However, it should be remembered the best defensive attack versus all offenses is to have the ability to execute a three- and four-deep principle, and use either one when the time arrives respectively against the good running or passing team, or when situations occur in a ball game. Diagrams 6-1 and 6-2 illustrate a three- and four-deep secondary.

IMPORTANCE OF DIFFERENT COVERAGES

It is necessary for the defensive coach to have at his disposal a number of defensive coverages in order to attack every offensive situation that may occur. There are numerous and varied defensive coverages a coach may employ. There are also many types and variations of zone, man-to-man and combinations that must be at hand for any offensive maneuver. These coverages should be prepared and ready before the beginning of the season and must be taught and drilled repeatedly in order for the defense(s) to be sound.

FORMATIONS AND ATTACKING THE FLATS AND WIDE-OUTS

In most cases, the offensive formations or sets a team presents will have a great deal to do with the types of defensive coverage that will be executed. If the offense uses closed formations with no flankers, slots or split ends, the defensive pass coverage will be prepared to halt any flat route hurting the defense. Since there are no wide-outs, there is little threat of a good pass receiver. Once the offense splits a man wide, the defense must be ready to vary or alter its defensive coverage if the situation arises. When two men are sent wide to one side by the offense, such as a wide-slot or twins formation, the defense must be prepared for this also. The last possibility can occur if the offense splits to both sides of the formation, such as a flanker on one side and a split end on the other. It may be difficult for the defense when one side displays a twins formation and the off-side has a split end also. Certain defensive coverages and an entire stunting game must be prepared for every situation that may occur. Usually wide receivers are excellent receivers, and they must be attacked properly in all situations.

When a team utilizes some form of wide-out, the flat areas become more vulnerable to a passing game. The defensive secondary should widen and spread out, and by accomplishing this, will force a better flat coverage by the defensive secondary. The defense must now look to the wide-out receiver and what he is attempting to accomplish. Also, the defense should keep an eye on the inside receiver going out or running a combination route. This differs a great deal when it is a closed formation (Wing-T) and all receivers are better contained by the defense. Certain pass combinations are limited because of the lateral distance between receivers, also.

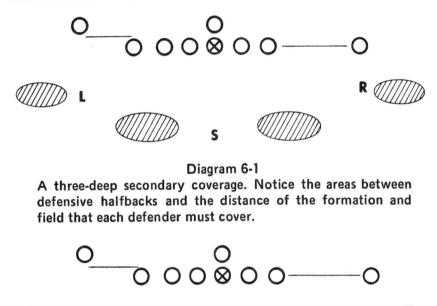

Diagram 6-1
A three-deep secondary coverage. Notice the areas between defensive halfbacks and the distance of the formation and field that each defender must cover.

Diagram 6-2
A four-deep secondary. Only one defensive linebacker is necessary versus five receivers. The areas of the field are cut down considerably versus the passing game because of the extra pass defender.

DIFFERENT OFFENSIVE PASS ROUTES IN THE FLATS

Pass routes in the flat areas can be executed by either the wide-out receiver or an offensive inside receiver; namely, a tight end, inside slot or halfback from his regular backfield position. Diagram 6-3 illustrates different pass routes in the flat areas that the defense will have to attack at one time or another if an offensive team is finding success. The defense will have to watch the flat and wide-out receivers and be able to cover such offensive pass routes as the quick-out, square-out, in, curl, quick slant, flat (quick-out by the inside receiver), seam, flat hook and swing from an offensive halfback. The outside screen is another possibility the defense must be prepared to cope with if it should occur. Of course, the action of the quarterback (sprint-out, throw-back, drop-back, etc.) will depend a great deal on the coverage that will be executed to attack these offensive threats.

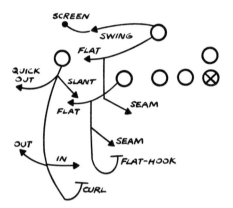

Diagram 6-3

ATTACKING THE WIDE-OUTS AND FLATS WITH DIFFERENT DEFENSES

It is very important that the defense have a variation or a different defense solely to attack a passing situation or a passing team. When the offensive running is not going well, they may attempt to go to the flats. If the offense is successful, the defense may have to execute a flat-oriented defense to cover just such a situation. In most cases, it is only necessary to station defenders in the flat (adjust them in the flat to meet the situation at hand) and attack the offense in any manner. Diagrams 6-4 through 6-6 illustrate different defenses with coverages in the flat areas. In all situations, the defense has to weaken themselves either up the middle, off-tackle or around the end, because of the removal of defenders out of the frontal areas and aligning them in the flat. However, the defense must be somewhat sound in order to play any other situation that may occur such as a draw, middle screen, quick trap up the middle, etc.

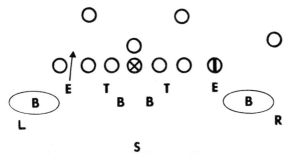

Diagram 6-4

A variation of the Split-4 versus a wide flanker. The outside linebackers adjust out. The off-tackle hole and containment becomes quite a chore for the defensive end. However, the flat is well-covered.

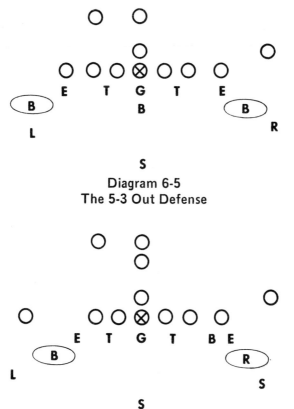

Diagram 6-5
The 5-3 Out Defense

Diagram 6-6

The Eagle-5 with a pre-rotate four deep and linebacker coverage in the flat to the split end side.

DEFENSIVE COVERAGE OF A FLANKER OR SLOT
BEFORE THE OFFENSIVE SNAP

There are numerous variations of a slot and flanker formation, usually dictated by the splits of both the inside and outside receiver. The defensive secondary and front alignment (ends and linebackers) should have definite split rules in terms of their alignments, stances, keys and responsibilities because one or more can alter as a result of the offensive formation. A flanker or wide-slot set usually has the wide receiver split about 7 to 15 yards from the inside receiver. Some of the formations the defense will encounter and should be prepared against are illustrated in Diagram 6-7. These include the tight and wide slot, twins and flanker formations.

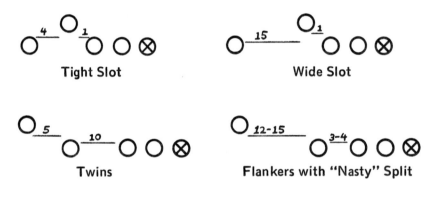

Diagram 6-7

Coverage before the ball is snapped is important, especially when the wide-out and the flat is being attacked by the offense during the course of a ball game. This is true if the wide-out man is a definite threat, because of his ability to catch and run with the football also. There are a few strategical defensive maneuvers versus the offense that can be accomplished and are listed as follows to combat such situations.

Install a New Defense

Install a new defense (as was explained) before the game to meet this threat, especially if the offensive opponent has shown through scouting and films that he has a good passing game with the wide-out or flat.

Pre-Rotate the Secondary

Pre-rotate the defensive secondary. This can easily be accomplished with the four-deep secondary, because it easily rotates, in most cases, after the snap of the football when playing zone coverage. The secondary will automatically go to a three-deep look with some type of coverage on the wide-out side. This is clearly indicated in Diagram 6-8. The defensive secondary can now execute three-deep or four-deep principles according to what the coach desires to accomplish.

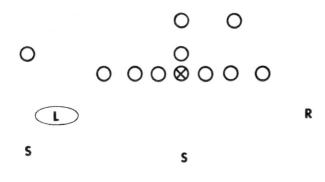

Any type of seven-man defensive coverage — 5-4, Pro-4, Eagle-5, etc.

Diagram 6-8

Different Defensive Coverages in the Flat

It is important, at this point, to list the different defensive alignments that can be utilized with any defender covering the flat area. This could be the cornerback rotated up as shown in Diagram 6-8, or it could be any linebacker or defensive end assigned to cover this area. Following are the different alignments that are utilized in attacking and covering the wide-out. Each has its own strengths and weaknesses and should only be employed to combat the many and varied situations that arise.

There are basically three defensive areas in which coverage can be used with numerous alignments in each. Diagram 6-9 illustrates the tight, walk-away and wide defensive attacking areas. Diagram 6-10 indicates the two defensive alignments by the defender covering the "tight" area. Alignment one is directly on the line of scrimmage.

This position allows the attack to either stunt hard inside for a good pass rush on the quarterback or allows him some maneuverability to the flat, especially on the curl route. However, he is not in the best alignment to cover any type of pattern executed by the offense. It does allow the defensive players inside of him to be more reckless in their pursuit for the running and passing game if the outside defender rushes. It must be remembered that any rush by this man automatically opens a few passing lanes to the wide-out receiver. However, the offense must cope with the rush. Position "two" shows the defender aligned approximately 1 to 2 yards outside the inside receiver and 3 yards off the line of scrimmage. This position places him in a better plane to cover the flat (as can be seen in the diagram) or come up and assist on any run off-tackle or outside. In this alignment, he may have the opportunity to rotate back in the other direction or cushion deeper if needed. In both positions (one and two), he is not able to harass the wide-out receiver.

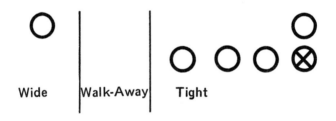

Wide   Walk-Away   Tight

Diagram 6-9

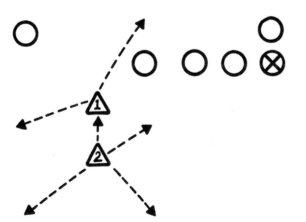

Diagram 6-10
The Tight Area

There are basically two positions a defender can align with in the walk-away area, and these are illustrated in Diagram 6-11. The number three alignment is used a great deal because of its proximity to both the inside and outside receiver. He is stationed approximately equidistant from either receiver and is approximately 4 yards off the football. This puts him in a good position to cover a quick flat, seam or quick slant from the wide receiver. He is in excellent position to cover any inside route by the wide man, such as a curl or in route, and any outside route by the inside receiver also. This alignment enables him to come up for any wide running play or sweep action. He can easily cushion deep on plays away from him and possibly invert to the deep middle according to the split of the offensive receiver.

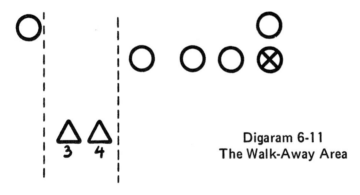

Digaram 6-11
The Walk-Away Area

The number four alignment is similar to the number three position; however, he will only split from the tight inside receiver no more than 6 yards. In other words, he will stay equally distant from the wide receiver up to a distance of 12 yards, but will align no farther, even if the wide-out splits 15-18 yards. This is done for a number of reasons. First, coverage of the wide receiver is important; however, the defense is not worried about the quick slant as much. It does not split the walk-away man out so far that he cannot cover any other inside pattern which may develop from the inside receiver or third man out. He can assist on cushion or invert deep middle even though the split receiver goes out more than 12 yards (15-19). The greater he has to split, as in position three, the more he cannot help in coverage down the middle or cushion area.

The wide area for the defensive coverages of the flat consists of six different alignments. As can be seen in Diagram 6-12, the number five, six and seven positions are basically the same, as are alignments eight, nine and ten. In position number five, the defender aligns directly on the line of scrimmage on the inside shoulder of the split receiver. He will be looking into the receiver with his inside foot forward and outside leg back. He will have his shoulders, chest and body facing out to him. On the movement of the wide-out, the defender will do everything he can to keep this man outside and force him away from the inside. Usually the receiver, if he is attempting to go inside, will get there, but it is the responsibility of the defender to harass him as much as possible. Once this has been accomplished, the defender will immediately look inside and attempt to read the pattern developing. If the outside receiver executes an inside route, the defender can look for any inside receiver to go out and vice versa. Of course this is only zone coverage in the flat, and other coverages will be explained later in the chapter.

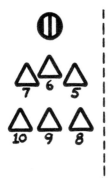

Diagram 6-12
The Wide Area

Aligning in the number six position will harass the wide-out receiver and accomplish about the same as the number five alignment. However, the receiver may be able to go inside and outside easier because of the head-up alignment. The number seven position places the defender on the outside shoulder of the receiver. His outside foot is forward, his inside leg is back and he is facing into the wide-out. This alignment is excellent because it takes the outside maneuvers away from the offensive split receiver and gives the defender an opportunity to look in to the quarterback from his alignment. He can now see the entire play develop and watch the inside receivers' routes, whether it be toward him or upfield. These three positions (five, six, seven) are excellent versus a good wide receiver and/or get good coverage for the wide patterns; i.e., square-out, out hook, etc. It is difficult to cover an inside route, but this can be taken away by another inside linebacker. The curl route can be covered from this alignment also. The defensive man from this position, however, cannot assist very much on a running play, unless it may be a sweep or a pitch-out on the option play.

The alignments of eight, nine and ten are similar, and was the case in the previous three positions discussed, and have the same strengths and weaknesses. However, the alignment differs in that they align approximately 4 yards off the receiver. Position eight is 4 yards in depth and aligned on the inside shoulder of the wide-out. Number nine alignment is head-up, while the number ten position stations on the outside shoulder. The strength of this alignment offers the defender a little extra time to see the release of the receiver and react to his move. He may have the opportunity to cover him a little longer and harass him more. He is, however, in good position to let this man go and cover any receiver from the inside coming to the flat. He may not be able to cover a seam route inside of him; however, he could not accomplish this from any other position aligned as wide either.

The three-deep secondary from an eight-man defensive front can pre-rotate, leaving a two-deep secondary look. When this is done, the defensive halfback must align wide and position either inside shoulder, head-up or outside shoulder of the wide-out receiver. He can now cover the flat area as was accomplished with the four-deep pre-rotation.

Bring a Defender Out from the Front Alignment

If the defense wants to cover a wide-out or the flat and does not desire to install a new defense or pre-rotate its secondary, it can bring out a defender from the defensive front, such as a linebacker or defensive end. When this is done, however, a great deal of support is lost up front for running and underneath coverage in the passing game. Aligning a defensive linebacker or end to cover this area can easily be accomplished from an eight-man defensive front. With this, the defense can still cover on seven offensive linemen. However, it does become difficult to accomplish from a nine-man front or four-deep secondary, unless there is a split receiver to the off-side. Certain defensive coverages become easier due to the lessening of down offensive blockers with a split receiver. Diagram 6-13 illustrates an example of a defensive end from a Wide-Tackle 6 (or eight-man front) Defense covering the flat area, while Diagram 6-14 shows a similar coverage from a nine-man front (5-4 Oklahoma Defense).

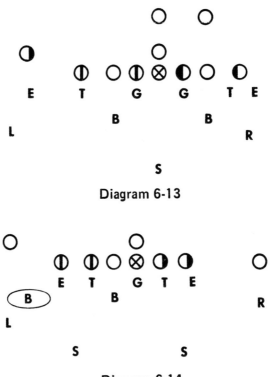

Diagram 6-13

Diagram 6-14

DEFENSIVE COVERAGE OF A SPLIT END BEFORE THE OFFENSIVE SNAP

Similar coverages on the flankerback or any wide receiver is approximately the same for a split end. However, there are certain priorities and variations.

Bring a Defender Out from the Front Alignment

Any time there is a split end, the defense usually covers with the front alignment first, because a blocker has been eliminated at the off-tackle area, and therefore a defender can assist on pass defense. The same basic defensive coverages can be utilized in the flat and on the wide-out receiver, as was explained previously in the tight, walk-away and wide areas. Diagram 6-15 illustrates these coverages versus a split end. The strengths and weaknesses of each position remain similar.

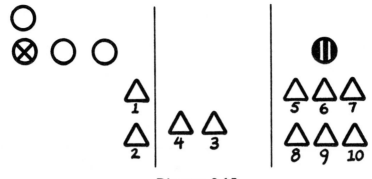

Diagram 6-15

Install a New Defense

An entire new defense to cover a good split end attack can be advised if it is warranted. This may be necessary for certain situations that arise or through the entire course of a ball game.

Pre-Rotate Secondary

Usually this is the last step in coverage of a split end and before the snap of the football. This is possible because the front alignment should be able to cope with the flat area. However, if an outside rush is desired on the split end side or a strong running game must be halted, then it may be necessary to pre-rotate in the flat to the split end, according to what is needed. The four-deep secondary can easily accomplish this and can still cover away from the pre-rotation. This is indicated in Diagram 6-16, utilizing the Eagle-5 Defense. A pre-rotation with the three-deep can be accomplished also; however,

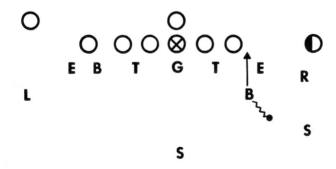

Diagram 6-16

certain defensive coverages must be executed away from the formation in order for the entire defense to be sound all around. Diagram 6-17 illustrates only one example of a Split-4 or eight-man defensive front with a pre-rotated secondary. Notice, however, that some type of defensive adjustment must be used to the strong side to combat the offensive set.

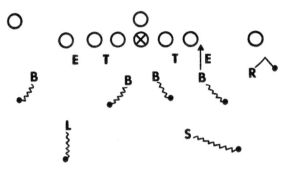

Diagram 6-17

DISGUISING DEFENSIVE COVERAGES

One of the most important factors in attacking the offensive passing game, especially at the flat area and wide-out receiver, is the effect of disguising defensive coverage. A coach should look to offensive thinking in order to understand the reasoning of disguise. An offensive team, when utilizing a passing game, has the option to execute three different methods. The quarterback and receivers can run the pattern called in the huddle and hope the pass succeeds, no matter what the defensive coverage being executed. The second method is to have the quarterback and possibly receivers read the secondary coverage *before* the snap of the football and alter the route or entire pattern if necessary. This can be accomplished quite easily, especially when double coverage is seen on one receiver before the snap. The quarterback can then throw to another receiver or check off to another play. The third way is to read and key the secondary coverage, not only before the snap of the football but also *after* the ball is hiked. This is a very sophisticated method of offensive attack, and it takes a great deal of time, patience and drilling to get the passing game to succeed. Once the offense has perfected this style of play, it can be a deadly attack to any defense.

It becomes important, therefore, for the defense to disguise the coverage before the snap of the football. For example, if the defense is executing a Pro-4 and they are encountering a good wide flanker, the secondary coverage could align in an invert look for as long as it takes the offensive team to get set and the quarterback to bark the signals. Once this has been done, the defense can quickly (with as much speed as possible) rotate to a three-deep and perform double coverage on the wide receiver (Diagram 6-17a). The only offensive maneuver which can be accomplished is the receivers can read the coverage after the snap or attempt to adjust the pattern or route very quickly. This becomes very difficult and can upset the offensive reading pass game. Disguising of the defensive coverage must be drilled during practice time and understood completely by the defenders who adjust. If they move late, and the ball is snapped before they reach their designated area of responsibility, it could result in an easy completion or possible touchdown if the defense is not prepared.

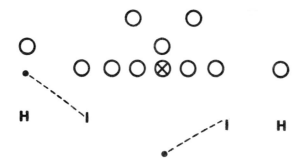

Diagram 6-17a
Rotating to a three deep before the snap of the football.

ATTACKING THE FLAT WITH A FOUR-DEEP SECONDARY

There are numerous schemes to attack the flat with the four-deep secondary. Two methods are explained, while the other means are discussed in detail in Chapter 11, "Attacking the Pro Strategical Passing Game." This is due to the intricate reading and keying details which must be utilized in attacking a reading offensive passing game. The defense must combat the offense by reading the maneuvers of the pass patterns, and attack with proper strategy. Turn to Chapter 11 for these coverages. The four methods of attack are as follows:

1. Rotation.
2. Invert.
3. Combination of Zone Coverage (Chapter 11).
4. Combination of Zone or Man Coverage (Chapter 11).

Rotational Coverage

The four-deep rotation can be utilized versus any offensive formation without difficulty. A few coaches believe that versus a wide-out situation a rotation cannot be executed, because of the difficulty of the defensive safety in covering the deep outside third of the field. However, this can be accomplished without any problem, and it is an excellent method in attacking any receiver entering the flat area. Diagram 6-18 illustrates the four-deep rotation. As the call is initiated to rotate or an offensive key becomes a factor, the cornerback, as shown, takes his initial step(s) and "hangs" in the flat to read the pattern that develops. If a receiver drives off the line, the defender will play him man-to-man in his zone. Once the receiver vacates the area, he should look for any other offensive man to come into that area. If his responsibility is to cushion when no receiver enters his zone, he must do so with caution. There is always the possibility of a screen. If a sprint action comes in his direction, he must stay in the flat area unless the passer crosses the line of scrimmage and decides to run the ball.

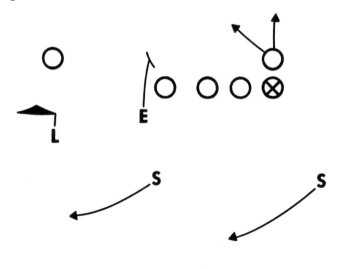

Diagram 6-18
Four-Deep Rotation

Invert Coverage

Most teams utilize the invert coverage versus wide-out receivers, but a few teams execute it versus any formation. The invert coverage is illustrated in Diagram 6-19. It is believed with this coverage that the deep outside third can be covered easier than rotation. The flat is more difficult to cover. However, if the invert defender is quick and doing his job correctly, he should be able to cover the flat without any trouble. One disadvantage is it may be difficult for the invert man to read the pattern as it develops while moving from inside-out rather than outside-in.

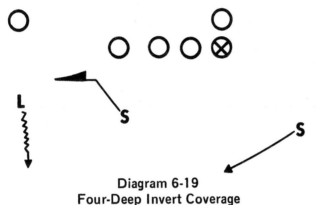

Diagram 6-19
Four-Deep Invert Coverage

He can be blocked quite easily from a crackback move by an outside wide-out also. His responsibilities remain similar to those of the cornerbacks in rotational coverage.

ATTACKING THE FLAT WITH THREE-DEEP ROTATION

The four methods of attacking the flat area with the four-deep secondary can be utilized with the three deep as well. The following are the coverages, with the last two reported in Chapter 11.

1. Rotational Coverage.
2. Invert Coverage.
3. Combination of Zone Coverage (Chapter 11).
4. Combination of Zone or Man Coverage (Chapter 11).

Three-Deep Rotational Coverages

Three-deep rotational coverage is just as effective in the flat area as the four deep. The only possible weakness that develops is in the deep areas, which is explained later in another chapter. The responsibilities of the defensive halfback on coverage in the flat zone are similar to the cornerback in four-deep rotation. Diagram 6-20 illustrates the three-deep rotation.

Three-Deep Invert Coverage

This type of coverage is not utilized to a great extent by many teams throughout the country. However, it can be effective coverage versus certain offensive patterns. It is difficult for the safety to cover the flat quickly, but he can better cover the inside routes. If the safety cheats over, the flat can be covered easier. The reasoning for this type of coverage is the defensive halfback can protect on the wide receiver easier and with more effectiveness. The off-side defensive halfback can now cover the other two-thirds of the field. An invert linebacker or other defender can also rotate into the deep middle as indicated in Diagram 6-21. The advantages and disadvantages of the three-deep invert are similar for the flat area, just as in the case of the four deep. The deep areas, as will be indicated later, are somewhat weakened.

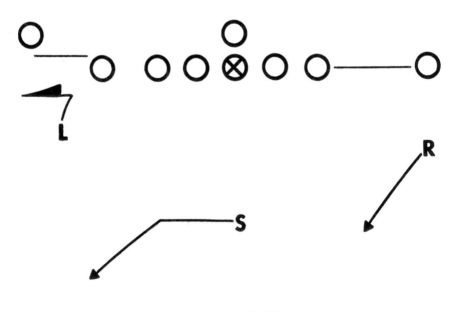

Diagram 6-20
Three-Deep Rotation

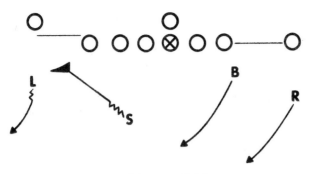

Diagram 6-21
Three-Deep Invert

ATTACKING THE WIDE-OUT RECEIVER WITH THREE- AND FOUR-DEEP SECONDARIES

A split receiver (if he has good ability and the quarterback can pass the ball to him) can be very successful versus any defensive team. It is necessary, if an offensive team has tendencies to pass the football on certain down-and-distance situations, or if it is a good passing team, that the defense prepares itself fully. The defense must play the wide receiver with any coverage it sees fit in order to halt or slow down this offensive attack. Strategy, with a great deal of planning, is very important and necessary. There are numerous methods in which to cover a good wide-out receiver, whether it be a flanker or split end. The following are ways to attack the wide-out receiver.

1. Bring a linebacker or other defender out on the wide receiver and play zone pass defense on him. This has already been fully explained.

2. Pre-rotate the defensive secondary and perform zone coverage. This has already been discussed in detail.

3. Play some type of man coverage underneath on the wide receiver with zone coverage deep.

4. If the defensive halfback is good, execute man-to-man on the wide-out. This, however, could prove to be difficult.

5. Play man-to-man coverage on the wide-out with zone underneath coverage, using linebackers or other defenders.

6. Play a special defense with two men executing man-to-man on the wide-out, if the receiver is exceptional. One will play him tough

while the other will defense him deep.

7.   Utilize a special defense where one man performs man-to-man only on the wide-out, while everyone else executes zone coverage.

Man Underneath Coverage with Deep Zone

This type of defense is excellent for man-to-man — and at the same time, it is being covered deep with some type of assistance. Man-to-man is being executed underneath while two defenders (sometimes one to the side of the wide-out dangerous receiver) remain deep for the long pass. The underneath defender plays the wide-out tough and attempts to knock the receiver off-balance as much as possible. He does not worry about the deep pass because he knows he is receiving assistance. Diagram 6-22 illustrates this type of coverage with the Pro-4 Defense. The three-deep secondary could easily employ this also.

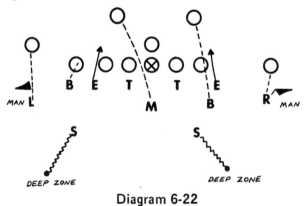

Diagram 6-22

One-on-One, Man-to-Man Coverage

This is a simple man-for-man coverage. Only when the defensive halfback is superior in all aspects to the offensive receiver is the defense good. The defensive halfback must be tough, quicker, faster, have the ability to catch the ball, be a good tackler if the receiver catches the football, etc. Since it is strictly man-for-man, there is nobody underneath or deep to assist on the wide-out.

Zone Underneath Coverage with Deep Man-to-Man

Diagram 6-23 illustrates zone underneath coverage with a defensive halfback playing man-to-man. In this instance, the defensive halfback does not have to bother about the short passing game, such as the out, curl, in, hook, etc. However, he must be concerned with the flag, post, streak, etc. patterns. Double coverage is being utilized short, but not long. The zone underneath defenders can now assist out on any swing, flat or screen type of pass ·

Two Man-to-Man Defenders (Special)

When two defenders are aligned on a wide-out receiver for man-to-man coverage, it places a great deal of strain on the other defensive players, because nine men must cover ten offensive people. However, if utilized in certain tactical situations, it may prove helpful. Usually, a special type of defense must be installed to accomplish this. As long as the defense is sound as to what the offense is doing in terms of formation, running and passing plays, it is good. The underneath defender can be tough and hit the receiver, for he realizes he is receiving assistance deep. This defender is mainly responsible for all the short, quick routes (slant, out, hook, curl, etc.). The deep defender covers long. In this coverage, both defenders play the receiver all over the field no matter what the pattern executed. Diagram 6-24 illustrates this coverage. A good way to cover is to place one defender on the inside shoulder, while the other man plays the outside shoulder as shown in the diagram.

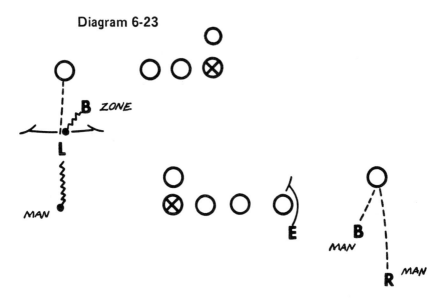

Diagram 6-23

Diagram 6-24

All Zone Coverage with One Defender Playing Man-to-Man (Special)

This is an excellent coverage to utilize versus a good wide receiver. Not only is man-to-man being used underneath, but also some type of zone is being employed. Zone coverage is being used deep for the long bomb also. In this situation, not only is zone taking the curls, ins, and hooks away, but a defensive man is playing the wide receiver short and long on all the patterns he attempts to run. Diagram 6-25 illustrates this coverage.

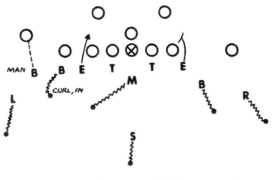

Diagram 6-25

ATTACKING OFFENSIVE PASS ROUTES

It is important that not only pass defensive strategy be used properly in attacking the offensive pass game, but also that defenders should use good techniques and fundamentals in covering the routes executed. Diagram 6-3 gave some examples of the pass routes that could be run in the flat area. Following are some of the skills necessary in covering the flat routes and patterns.

Covering the Flat Route

When a man is stationed in the walk-away position or rotates up to cover the flat, he must look for the pattern to be executed. The first maneuver he should notice is the inside receiver's route. If it is to be to the outside immediately (flat cut), usually the outside receiver's route will be inside. Since the flat route is to be covered, the defender should execute his initial movements, remain low and attempt to stay on the outside shoulder of the receiver. This position is good, because if the pass is thrown, the receiver cannot run away from the defender. At the same time, the defender can go through the outside shoulder of the receiver to the football. If for some reason the defender misses the ball and the receiver catches it, he will be at least forced inside so other pass defenders will be able to assist. If the defender goes through the inside shoulder of the receiver and misses the offensive man, he can now sprint down the sideline and a longer pursuit is needed by the entire defensive unit.

Covering the Swing Route

This offensive cut can be utilized on almost any pattern, especially when the wide receivers go inside. This, however, is not a standard rule. The defender should hang in the flat or this route. He should not attempt to come up at a bad angle so if the ball were caught he would be approaching the receiver from the "inside shoulder-out." Once the defender reads the route, he should run parallel to it and maintain a good relationship with the receiver also. This is illustrated in Diagram 6-26. It is important to go through the outside shoulder of the receiver and force him into the inside if possible.

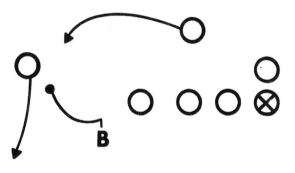

Diagram 6-26

Covering a Seam Route

This can only be accomplished if the defender is either in a tight or walk-away position, where he can go out and cover the flat cut but be in a position to stop his progression when the receiver moves upfield. The defender should stay low — and, as he sprints to cover the seam, he should keep his shoulders and body facing the quarterback with his eyes on the ball, and, at the same time, keep peripheral vision on the receiver's route. In this instance, he will be playing underneath coverage and should attempt to harass the receiver with his hands and body.

Covering "Out Routes" by a Wide Receiver

To cover any route by a wide-out, it is almost necessary that the defender be either stationed on the split man or some form of rotation be used where the defender is coming up from outside-in. When this is accomplished, the defender can execute underneath coverage between the passer and the receiver. Any other coverage, such as a tight or walk-away position, would be very difficult to cover in the flat.

Covering "In Routes" from a Wide Receiver

The in route can usually be taken away from the wide-out when a defender is stationed on the inside of him. This can be done from the walk-away position at best, but it may also be accomplished from the tight position. Rotation can assist, but an invert coverage may be more helpful. In all cases, it is important for the underneath defenders to flow between the passer and the receiver, while the secondary defenders attempt to go through the outside shoulder of the receiver so as to force him to run inside toward the pursuit of the defense.

7

Attacking
the Inside Receivers
and Hook Areas

M ost defensive coaches position their best secondary defenders in pass coverage on the split ends and flankers. This reasoning, of course, is excellent because many offensive-minded coaches place their best personnel in these positions. One strategical idea that only a few offensive coaches are accomplishing at present, especially with the passing game, is stationing the best receivers "inside" the flankers and split ends. These coaches will align these receivers in a more advantageous position, such as at tight end or in the backfield. The reasoning is obvious. The offense is placing its better personnel against a possible weaker safety(s) and/or linebackers. Diagram 7-1 illustrates this offensive maneuver versus a four-deep defensive situation. The defensive coach could imagine what weaknesses could develop if strictly a three-deep defense, such as the Split 4-4, Wide-Tackle 6, 5-3, etc., were employed. Two linebackers would be responsible for the offensive halfbacks.

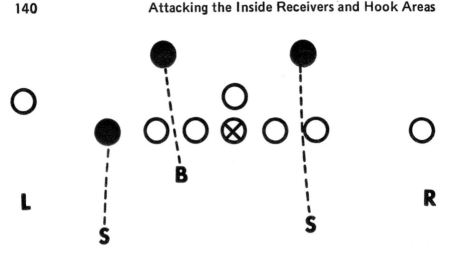

Diagram 7-1

This thought is only being mentioned, because if a coach must face a passing attack where the offensive receivers are good, he must have his defensive scheme prepared for this type of set-up. If he is employing a three-deep secondary with underneath linebacker coverage, he must have good personnel in these positions to cover good offensive backs and possibly a quick and fast tight end or slotback. A four-deep secondary is better equipped against a good inside passing attack because less linebacker coverage is necessary. However, the football coach must have key personnel responsible for these receivers if they are better than the wide-outs.

THE VARIED INSIDE RECEIVERS

Offensive formations have a good deal to do with the type of inside receivers there are and how each must be attacked. Offensive running routes utilized by these receivers can usually be known well in advance through the use of scouting, films, etc. The defensive attack of formations, field position, personnel etc. will, in numerous cases, formulize what the defensive coach will utilize in covering offensive patterns. For example, an inside receiver on the line of scrimmage could be a tight end or a slotback, and each could be maneuvered along the line in an attempt to get certain defensive adjustments. Diagram 7-2a indicates different slotback adjustments while 7-2b illustrates tight end alignments. This is indicated because of two main reasons.

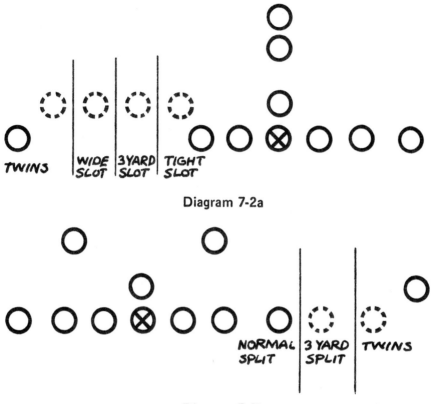

Diagram 7-2a

Diagram 7-2b

1. The different alignments can signify various coverages, because only certain offensive plays and/or sequences can be accomplished (both running and passing) from each formation.

2. Different personnel are being utilized for the inside receiver. One is a tight end who is usually a better blocker but not as quick or as good a receiver. The slotback, however, is probably faster and more apt to be a better offensive receiver.

Field position is another important factor of consideration in coverage of inside receivers. Defensive linebackers can cover a team better on a hash-mark when the receivers run routes to the sideline. The area for the pass route is extensively diminished, and both zone and man-to-man coverage is easier to accomplish. However, when routes are run to the field, the coach must have his linebackers and secondary prepared to cover the patterns executed also.

The defensive coach must prepare his players to attack different and varied slots, tight ends, wingbacks, flankers and split ends coming across, fullbacks and tailbacks running out of the backfield, delay tactics over the middle, etc. Diagram 7-3 illustrates a few of these maneuvers.

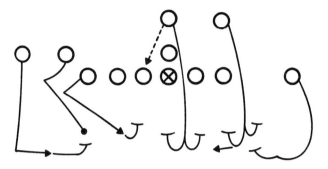

Diagram 7-3

LINEBACKER COVERAGE

When attacking the varied offensive games a defense must face from game to game, it is important to have good and proper linebacker coverage. This must be accomplished if linebackers play zone and cover areas, or when they execute man-to-man techniques. The number of linebackers a coach utilizes in his underneath coverage depends upon the defense being used. If, for example, a defensive coach uses a 7-1 defensive alignment, he will not get much linebacker coverage underneath using one linebacker. Most defensive coaches utilize two-, three- and four-man linebackers in their

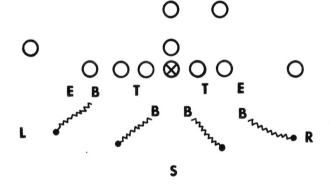

Diagram 7-4

underneath coverage. The best all-around coverage is usually a four-deep secondary with a three-linebacker set-up, or a three-deep secondary with a four-linebacker combination. Diagram 7-4 illustrates the Split-4 coverage, while Diagram 7-5 shows the Pro-4. It must be readily understood, however, that coverage of inside receivers and hook areas with zone can be accomplished to a greater degree of success with utilization of four linebackers rather than three.

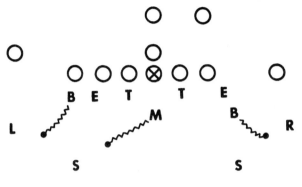

Diagram 7-5

ATTACKING INSIDE RECEIVERS COMING OFF THE LINE OF SCRIMMAGE

When a defensive linebacker is stationed on the line of scrimmage and is responsible for a tight end, it is important for him to execute all the necessary skills and techniques of stance, execution, delivery of blow, reading, keying, etc. Preventing the tight end from releasing easily is important. The linebacker must stay low, deliver the blow into the receiver and attempt to control him for just a moment in order to read run or pass. Once pass is recognized and the receiver releases, the linebacker should attempt, at the least, to deliver another blow, hoping to knock him off his course. A good receiver will try to get back on his proper route, and this is when the linebacker has the opportunity to hit the receiver again. The linebacker can harass the receiver as much as he desires as long as the ball is not in the air. He should try to accomplish this, and at the same instant, carry out his responsibilities, for the defense called.

If offensive backs are to be covered, either in man or zone, different techniques can be used. If a linebacker has protection behind him — i.e., defensive safeties, etc. — he can attack the offensive back with a little more authority. When covering an offensive back, it is necessary to hit him *before* he makes his cut inside or outside. This can only be accomplished if the linebacker attacks the back aggressively and quickly. To throw a good back off-stride, the linebacker should attempt to hit him squarely and *not* from the side. Diagram 7-6 illustrates this point very vividly. To achieve good contact with the offensive back, the linebacker should move quickly and take an angle that will position himself head-to-head with his opponent. This teaching technique will assure *proper contact* with the receiver, and not a slight shove which may result.

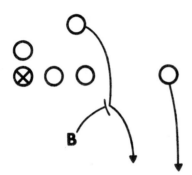

Only shoves defender
in one direction.

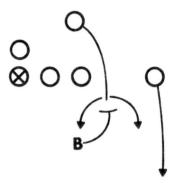

Forces the receiver to
commit inside or outside.

Diagram 7-6

If the defensive linebacker must cover an offensive back with no secondary assistance, it is quite obvious this technique cannot be employed. The linebacker must drop from the line to keep his depth if the offensive halfback is not to outrun him on a long pass. If this type of coverage is being utilized, then good pressure from stunts must be accomplished to compensate for one-on-one situations.

DEFENSES FOR THE INSIDE GAME

If a defense is being attacked in the hook areas and by the inside receivers, other defenses can be utilized. Without discussing the stunting game, which usually dictates a form of man-to-man principles, other defensive sets can be employed before the snap of the football. To accomplish good linebacker coverage underneath, it is necessary to employ a three- or four-man defensive rush on the passer.

Diagram 7-7 illustrates a simple adjustment from the Split-4 Defense. The inside linebacker adjusts to the outside eye of the offensive tackle while the defensive tackle moves inside over the guard. The linebacker is in a better alignment to attack the hook area and/or the tight end, or any inside receiver coming out of the backfield. This could be accomplished on both sides of the offensive center and gives an appearance of a Wide-Tackle 6 Defense. Diagram 7-8 indicates the 4-4 Tandem Defense which positions the outside linebackers off the line of scrimmage. If any defense were being attacked inside, the four linebackers shown in this alignment would be in excellent areas to cover and take away this part of the offensive game.

While Diagram 7-7 and 7-8 were illustrations from the three-deep defense, Diagram 7-9 indicates a simple adjustment from the Pro-4 Defense. Diagram 7-10 shows a triple stack that can be easily utilized from either the Pro-4 or 5-4 Defense. A three- or four-man pass rush can be employed.

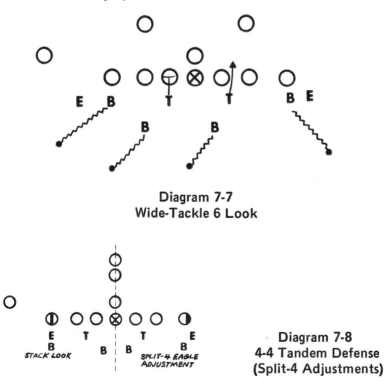

Diagram 7-7
Wide-Tackle 6 Look

Diagram 7-8
4-4 Tandem Defense
(Split-4 Adjustments)

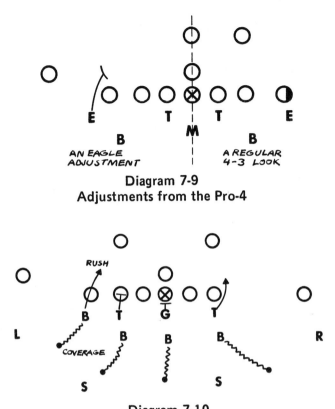

Diagram 7-9
Adjustments from the Pro-4

Diagram 7-10
The Triple Stack Look
An excellent coverage versus the pass since there are four
linebackers and four deep defenders.

UTILIZING ZONE COVERAGE

It is important to stress what the offense is aiming to accomplish with the passing game inside. The passes thrown inside usually initiate from either semi-sprint or roll action, drop-back or play action fakes. A strictly sprint-out operation will not effectively beset a team inside. It is desirable for the defensive coverage to attack the *offensive patterns* and not always go to the zone and protect it. Diagram 7-11 illustrates the Split-4 inside dropping zone. The outside linebackers are getting depth and width. If the inside receivers are proceeding to the flat and the outside linebackers do not have flat responsibility, because of the three-deep rotational coverage, the linebackers, therefore, should expect an inside route by the outside wide-out. This could be a curl, hook, square-in, etc. If the inside receiver drives straight upfield, the outside linebacker should be alert for a quick inside pattern by the outside receiver or some other type of route by the inside slot or tight end. The inside linebacker can immediately scan to both the tight end, slot and/or a possible route from an offensive back. The inside linebacker should get enough depth so as to cover the routes utilized. The exact depth of the offensive receivers should be practiced and drilled so linebackers are aware of their depth-and-width position.

Diagrams 7-12 and 7-13 indicate inside zone coverage with the Pro-4 and the 5-4 Defense. As can be seen, a four-linebacker defense can attack short easier than either a two- or three-linebacker defense. When executing zone in this situation, a three-deep secondary can rotate forward for an extra defender underneath. Consult Chapter 11, "Attacking the Pro Strategical Passing Game," for a better insight on defending offensive patterns.

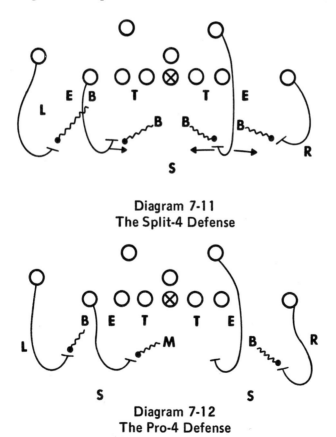

Diagram 7-11
The Split-4 Defense

Diagram 7-12
The Pro-4 Defense

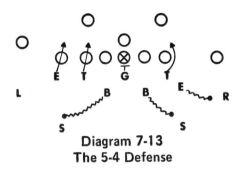

Diagram 7-13
The 5-4 Defense

An excellent underneath zone coverage can be employed from either the three- or four-deep defense. Five areas are secured underneath while a two-deep zone is employed (Diagrams 7-14 and 7-15). This places a great deal of pressure upon an offense, especially if they cannot connect on a receiver deep. The defensive pass coverage can either be executed tight or loose, and can be "aligned in" directly before the snap of the football or after the ball is put into play.

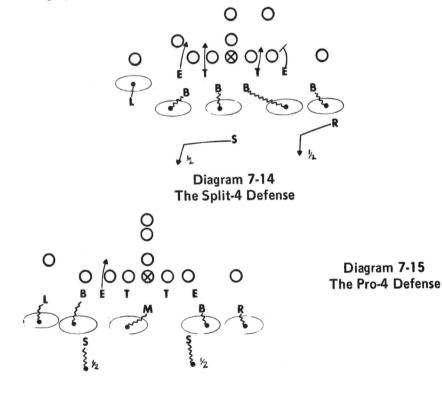

Diagram 7-14
The Split-4 Defense

Diagram 7-15
The Pro-4 Defense

MAN-TO-MAN COVERAGE

Man-to-man coverage can be utilized quite easily with some method of stunting or a defensive maneuver. With a four-deep secondary, the two defensive safeties and one linebacker are necessary for this coverage (Diagram 7-16). However, using man-to-man principles with a three-deep secondary requires two linebackers and one defensive safety (Diagram 7-17). In these two situations, the three-deep secondary is a weaker defense because of the extra linebacker needed for pass protection. Pressure is more important in this situation than from a four-spoke defense.

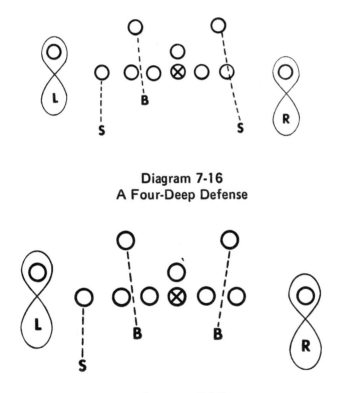

Diagram 7-16
A Four-Deep Defense

Diagram 7-17
A Three-Deep Defense

Inside-Outside Man-to-Man Versus Inside Receivers

Linebackers alone or with defensive safeties can utilize various combination inside-outside man-to-man defenses. These defensive coverages are utilized because certain inside receivers may be quicker or better receivers and/or certain patterns executed by the offense may be difficult to cover. Diagram 7-18 illustrates two linebackers playing the strong-side offensive halfback and the weakside halfback inside-outside from a Split-4 Defense. A defensive safety and linebacker are indicated in Diagram 7-19 on a slotback. Also, a linebacker and defensive end are illustrated on the split end side from a 5-4 Defense.

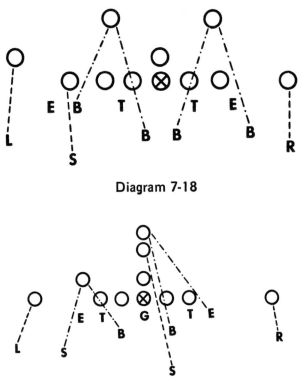

Diagram 7-18

Diagram 7-19

   It is important to realize that once a receiver makes his break either inside or outside, the other defender is free to play zone or assist on another receiver running into the area. A defensive safety and linebacker combination is effective. If the safety gets free, he can now become a "free safety" and assist on any receiver who may release deep.

MAN-TO-MAN WITH FREE SAFETY COVERAGE

Man-to-man linebacker coverage can be utilized with one or two free safeties involved for deep pass protection. A regular rush is usually the case or other forms of pressure can be used. The strength of this coverage is due to the fact that underneath linebacker performance can be played very tough and aggressive versus the offensive receivers. Diagram 7-20 indicates a two-deep zone with underneath man-to-man coverage. If a particular inside receiver is quick and fast and happens to be relatively tough to cover, an inside-outside approach can be employed by the linebackers. Possible double coverage with a deep free safety (Diagram 7-21) is excellent also.

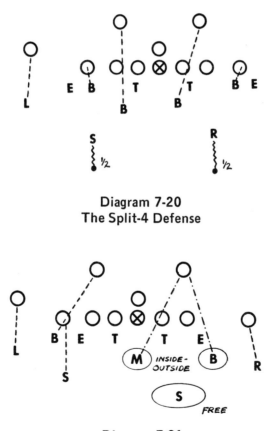

Diagram 7-20
The Split-4 Defense

Diagram 7-21
The Pro-4 Defense

MAN-TO-MAN WITH UNDERNEATH ZONE COVERAGE

While the deep zone protection was illustrated with underneath man-to-man, one of the strongest coverages versus inside receivers is utilizing man-to-man with the deep secondary while the linebackers cover zones. This coverage gives good man-to-man, but, at the same time, linebackers can be reading patterns and forming protection in their respective areas. Diagram 7-22 illustrates man-to-man on the inside receivers. However, the inside hook and short areas are well-protected. While the Pro-4 Defense is shown, this pass coverage can be utilized by both the Split-4 and the 5-4 Defense as well.

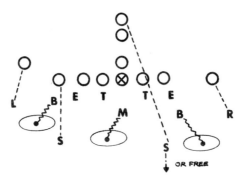

Diagram 7-22

COVERING THE INSIDE RECEIVERS WITH
SPECIAL DEFENSES

As has been mentioned previously, some inside receivers are exceptional and other pass coverages may be necessary. These are usually special defenses that are designed for a particular player or two. This usually comprises some form of double coverage or a zone defense with a defender covering the receiver man-to-man.

As an example, a rather simple double coverage is shown in Diagram 7-23 from a Split-4 Defense. The outside and inside linebacker key on the halfback. When he attempts to release, he is hit hard and vigorously by the outside linebacker. The inside linebacker maneuvers quickly for additional coverage. A free safety is utilized as indicated. However, he could pick up one of the inside receivers and release one of the other linebackers for additional pass rushing.

Diagram 7-24 illustrates another special defensive coverage. While a four-deep secondary is used, this can easily be accomplished with a three-deep secondary also. The defense plays basically zone, but the strong-side defensive safety releases from the coverage and jumps upon the tight end or second inside receiver on the line. He executes a tough man-to-man technique all over the field on the receiver.

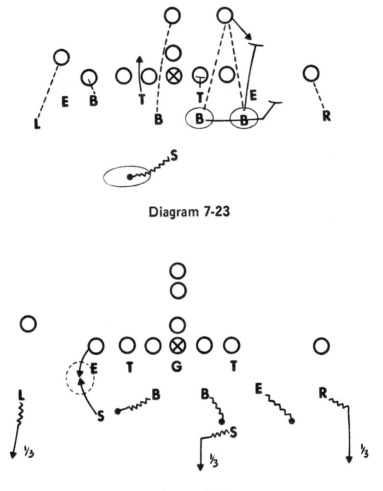

Diagram 7-23

Diagram 7-24

These defenses are but two examples of what can be accomplished with pass coverage on good offensive pass receivers. A number of different and varied coverages could be utilized. It is necessary for the coach to be totally prepared for any type of passing game and have his defense prepared for attack when the time arrives.

8

Attacking
the Deep Areas

The deep completed pass thrown by the offense can spoil a good defensive performance. Many defensive teams can work all afternoon and get hurt by the long "bomb." It is very important for the defensive coach to be prepared, at all times, for situations that may occur when the offensive team desires to strike at the deep secondary coverage. There have been so many instances, which have been seen in college and professional football, where teams have little time remaining in the half or game and complete the long pass either for a desirable gain or a touchdown.

There are numerous instances during a season where a football coach will come up against a good passing team or a quarterback who can throw long. Usually these teams have excellent receivers who normally can catch a ball in a crowd. To be ready, the defense must attack at the source of the offense. The defense must be prepared to attack in as many various ways as possible, not only the long pass but also the good receivers as well.

It is necessary for the coach to know the type of long patterns a team desires to throw or which routes have had the most success versus other defenses. These routes can include the fly, post, flag, down-and-up, hook-and-go, etc.

Drilling versus these routes can considerably assist a secondary defender in knowing and reacting to the offensive patterns being executed.

ATTACKING THE LONG PASS

There are many and varied methods to attack a passing team and/or situations. A defense should be totally prepared for the strategical attack to combat such threats. It is not possible to have one or two defenses and tactically hope that these will halt an offense. There are too many styles of offensive threats, such as the type of offense being employed and the personnel used in certain positions for that particular offense, for a defense to have only one or two defenses. A team that uses the drop-back passing game with power type running is entirely different than one showing sprint-out and a triple option look. This is why it is totally necessary to have a varied defensive attack versus a long and deep passing team to counteract any offensive threat. To accomplish these goals, there are many defensive attacks which can be used. The following are a few of the methods that a defense should be prepared to have at its disposal versus the long pass:

1. *Playing Normal Defensive Secondary Play Well.* A team should be totally drilled and prepared for any long pass. A secondary defender should never leave his deep zone until after the ball is thrown.

2. *Having Man-to-Man Coverage with a Free Safety.* While many teams execute man-to-man well, it is necessary to have a free safety who can roam and cover deep for added protection.

3. *Utilizing Zone with a Free Safety.* Numerous teams do not use a free safety with zone coverage. However, it is an excellent coverage against a long-styled passer.

4. *Employ Double Coverage Against an Excellent Receiver.* Putting two defenders on one man may be necessary against a long-threat receiver.

5. *A Three-Man Rush Is Good.* When eight defenders can be utilized to cover the zones, it gives the defense a well-balanced secondary coverage.

6. *Adding Pressure for a Pass Rush.* A good pass rush is necessary at times and can throw an offense for a sizable loss in some instances.

7. *Strategy Is Most Important.* Utilizing the right defense at the right

time is very necessary against a good passing team. When to rush, when not to rush, playing man, executing zone or a combination of each, all play important roles in attacking the deep passing game.

SECONDARY PLAY

The defense must be fully prepared when facing a good passing offense. When an offense or situation arises, and the long bomb is expected, it is necessary for the secondary defenders to cover their respective men or zones well. This cannot be a time to let up, because this is probably the easiest method an offense can utilize to score a touchdown or secure a long gain.

Alignment

The alignment of the defenders in the defense called is important. Since good depth and width is needed, it may do well for them to take one or two steps back in order to gain position on their receivers.

Initial Execution

Once the football has been snapped, quick initial steps backward to get position and read the offensive play should be carried out. Keeping low and alert to the developments of the offensive action should be accomplished.

Responsibilities

As soon as the play has been read by the defenders, reaction to their responsibilities must be accomplished quickly and effectively. Whether it be man-to-man or some form of zone coverage, the defenders should provide a little more "cushion" between the receivers and themselves, so the responsibilities of halting any long pass can be made easier. The position of the football is important for strategy and the defenders' execution. What yardline and the location of the hash-mark − i.e., left, middle and right − will determine to a great extent how the defenders play the defense called and the type of receivers they are defending against. Once the ball is in the air, the defenders should react as quickly as possible to the area. The more defenders moving to the ball, the better chance there exists of an interception or of knocking the ball to the ground. If the ball is ever caught, there is a better opportunity to tackle the receiver and stop him for little gain if the defenders swarm to the ball.

DISGUISING DEFENSES

Since many good and well-balanced passing offenses instruct their quarterbacks, backs, flankers and ends to key and read defensive secondary coverages before and after the snap of the football, it is necessary for the defenders to attack this phase of the game. To accomplish this, the defense, especially before the offensive snap, should align or possibly disguise in some way the coverage to be employed. For example, a three-deep defensive secondary could position themselves into a man-to-man look, but once the ball is put into action, revert into a zone coverage (Diagram 8-1). The same can hold true indicating a zone look, but using a man-to-man coverage. When a passer can throw the ball long with accuracy, disguising of secondary play is an important aspect of proper defensive attack.

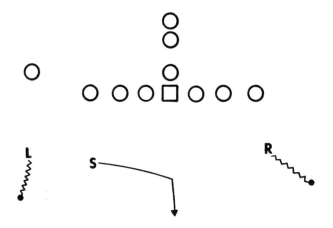

Diagram 8-1
The safety (S) aligns over the offensive tight end, indicating man-to-man coverage. However, once the ball is snapped, he runs to zone coverage.

With the secondary defensive attack, three- and four-deep pass coverages will be discussed. Since the Pro-4 and the 5-4 Defense utilize four-deep principles, these coverages will be similar. The three-deep attack is used by any eight-man front defense, including the Split-4, Wide Tackle 6, 5-3, etc.

EMPLOYING THE TWO-DEEP ZONE

The two-deep zone concept has already been discussed. Versus the deep passing game, the man-to-man underneath coverage is best, because as the receivers run their routes deep, and the long ball is thrown, there will be at least two to three defenders around the football (Diagram 8-2). The underneath zone with two safeties does not assist as well as man coverage. This is obvious. The underneath zone defenders stop in their short areas and do not go deep even though receivers may run long.

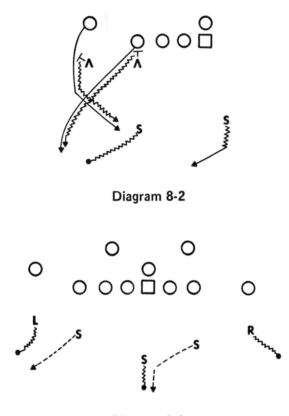

Diagram 8-2

Diagram 8-3

THE THREE-DEEP VERSUS THE FOUR-DEEP SECONDARY

For attacking the offensive passing game, the three-deep may be considered a better secondary coverage than a four-spoke rotational or invert defense. This is quite obvious, because three-deep defenders are positioned in their zone coverage and cannot be beaten as well on the quick, long passes. The four spoke, however, must rotate or utilize some form of invert coverage to align in three deep. This can readily be seen in Diagram 8-3 with the three- and four-deep principles.

FOUR-DEEP ZONE COVERAGE

If the defense wants to concede one of the flat areas, because of the passing situation or style of offensive game, the four-man umbrella secondary does not have to rotate. It can remain four across, and each defensive halfback will only cover one-quarter of the field, as shown in Diagram 8-4. Each defender has less area of coverage and responsibility, and this type coverage grants added protection deep.

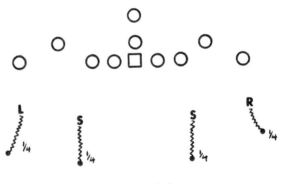

Diagram 8-4

MAN-TO-MAN DEFENSES

It is not a good idea to utilize complete man-to-man defense versus a long-passing team. If any one receiver is beaten deep and the ball is delivered to him, no assistance can be given by the other defenders. They are attempting to cover their respective men, and if the receivers are running long, they cannot assist on coverage.

UTILIZING MAN-TO-MAN WITH A FREE SAFETY

Man-to-man coverage can be employed with one free safety to cover deep on any long pass from either three- or four-spoke coverages. Usually a free safety will emphasize responsibility on the side of a formation or on certain receivers. However, he has the advantage of keeping his eyes, not only on the pattern executed, but on the passer as well. Once the ball is released, he can sprint to it and considerably support the defender covering the receiver. It is necessary that the free safety align or get to his depth position in order to fulfill his assignment of the defense. He cannot be caught flat-footed, especially on any long pass. Diagrams 8-5 and 8-6 illustrate man-to-man coverages with a free safety from the Split-4 and the Pro-4 Defense. As can be seen from these coverages, a good four-man rush can be executed by the defense. Any placement of the linebackers can be accomplished in order to get good man-to-man coverage. An extra linebacker is shown free also. He is in excellent position to either play zone or rush the passer.

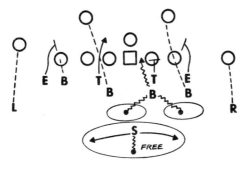

Diagram 8-5

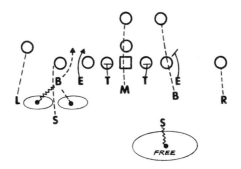

Diagram 8-6

Double Coverage with a Free Safety

If an offensive team has an excellent receiver, double coverage of this threat is good with the free safety attack (Diagram 8-7). Man-to-man is used with the other defenders, and a good four-man rush is carried out on the passer. Double coverage can be employed on any receiver, whether he is positioned as a flanker, split end, tight end, tailback, fullback, etc. It can be one of the better defensive attacks versus a good receiver and a long passing team.

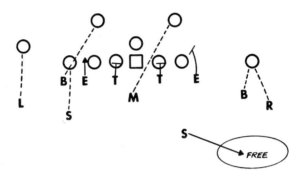

Diagram 8-7

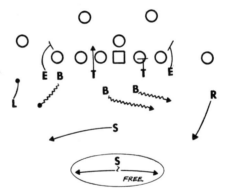

Diagram 8-8
A Three Deep with Rotation Indicated

THE THREE-ONE PREVENT ZONE

The three-one secondary zone is designed especially for the long pass. It is an excellent coverage because the three defenders can remain in a three deep with an extra defensive safety aligned behind for support. The three deep can rotate and utilize other coverages with the free safety also. Actually, any defensive alignment can be employed up front. Diagram 8-8 illustrates this coverage. The free safety can align anywhere from 18 to 25 yards in depth. He should not play any patterns but must go to the ball once it is in the air. However, he should never lose sight of the fact that if he goes directly for the football, the offensive receiver cannot gain position on him. From his depth of alignment, the free safety should be able to cover the field and play the ball. Usually the underneath coverage will be determined by the alignments and pass rush employed.

ATTACKING WITH THE FOUR-ONE PREVENT ZONE

In definite passing situations, a four-one zone defensive attack can be utilized versus the long passing zone. There are numerous and varied secondary coverages that can be employed. One example is a simple rotation, as shown in Diagram 8-9. Since five-deep defenders are used, only six defensive linemen and linebackers are available. This attack is especially good when the offense splits an end. There are, then, six up-front defenders versus six offensive linemen. Any defensive look can be accomplished from the Pro 4-3, 5-4, 5-Eagle, etc.

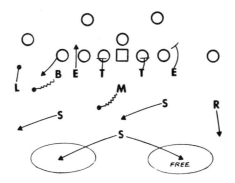

Diagram 8-9

Although rotation is indicated to a flanker-tight end, rotational coverage can be utilized toward the split end also. The free deep fifth safety usually aligns 25 yards in depth. His job or responsibility can be changed from situation to situation and game by game. For example, if the split end is a dangerous receiver, the secondary can rotate in his direction on the drop-back pass, and the free safety can maneuver his alignment and responsibility toward him and his area of the field. Other four-deep coverages can easily be utilized to meet the different offensive threats that may occur. Employing invert zone, man-to-man with the free safety are just two examples.

EMPLOYING THE FIVE ROTATE OR INVERT COVERAGE

The five-deep secondary attack can easily be accomplished from any defensive alignment. The purpose of the coverage is to get four defenders deep to cover their respective quarter of the field, and at the same time to be able to cover the flat toward the strength of the passing game (Diagram 8-10). Since there are six defensive players up front, it is important for these men to be prepared for any running threat and/or draws and screens. Any defensive alignment can be used for this purpose. Invert secondary coverage can be utilized also. The outside halfbacks (L and R) would change responsibility with the inside halfbacks (H's). If this were to be accomplished to a side of the formation, one of the halfbacks would respond to the flat, while the outside halfback would be responsible for the deep outside quarter of the field.

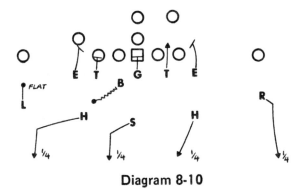

Diagram 8-10

THREE-MAN DEFENSIVE RUSHES

Rushing a passing game with three players is usually not done until either at the end of a half or a game, with the defenders leading. Eight people cover the zone areas. The three rushers are used not as pressure, but for security against any scramble by the quarterback. The defense knows the offense will pass the ball and possibly complete it. However, all four short zones and the four-deep areas are completely covered (Diagram 8-11). The secondary is very conscious of the long pass and will automatically align deeper and be alert for this threat. Any defensive alignment and rushing lane can be used. Man-to-man coverage underneath with four men, or utilizing some form of double coverage on a good receiver, can also be employed.

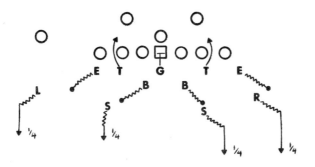

Diagram 8-11

ATTACKING WITH PRESSURE

As the old saying goes, "The best pass rush is the best pass defense." This can be true, especially when the offensive pass protection breaks down or is not as good as the defensive rush. To place pressure on the long passing game, it usually requires man-to-man secondary coverage. However, it is wise to include a free safety. This sort of coverage is excellent because of three important reasons. First, there is at least a six- or seven-man rush executed against the offense; second, tight man-to-man coverage is utilized on the various receivers and, third, a free safety is being utilized for the long pass.

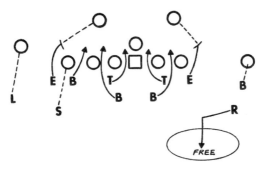

Diagram 8-12
A Seven-Man Rush from the Split-4 Defense

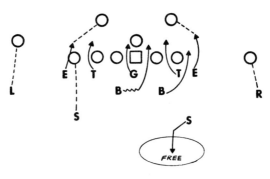

Diagram 8-13
A Seven-Man Rush from the 5-4 Defense

Any defensive alignment can be utilized from three-and four-deep secondaries. Diagrams 8-12 and 8-13 indicate two examples of the Split-4 and the 5-4 Defense. As can be seen, the defensive ends play an important role in the coverage. Once they have executed their initial execution and read it as a pass, they will rush the passer and key their respective men. If the receiver releases for a pass, the ends will cover them out of the backfield. However, if the backs remain for pass protection, the ends will continue on for the passer. They must, however, be alert for any type of screen.

9

Attacking
the Triple Option

The triple option offense is one of the most potent and devastating games. Its maneuverability along the line of scrimmage has been a nightmare for many defenses. There are numerous major college football teams in the country that have rolled up yardage and have shattered many yardage and scoring records. To stop the triple

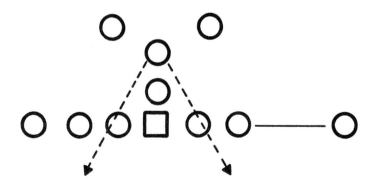

The Wishbone-T
Diagram 9-1

The Pro Look
Diagram 9-1 (cont.)

option, therefore, the defense must be thoroughly knowledgeable of the principles and concepts behind the offense.

The triple option can be executed from almost any formation. However, the most often used and discussed formations have been the Wishbone-T and/or Pro (flanker-split end variation). (See Diagram 9-1.) The offense aspires to exploit the defense by reading the different maneuvers of the forward alignment and getting the ball to one of three possible ball-carriers; i.e., dive back, quarterback or pitch man.

When new and varied offenses come along every few years, it usually takes time for defenses to defend them. Defensive alignments with certain stunts and/or slanting lines must be developed, to not only attack, but also realize success. This is true for the triple option. The triple option can be drastically reduced as long as defenses are drilled and tactical plans are intelligently made.

Personnel is always a factor. Many triple option teams have success, because usually the better-skilled athlete is positioned at quarterback and halfback. Since the quarterback reads the maneuvers of the defensive reactions, it is extremely necessary for the defensive personnel to read the offense also. It is important that each position not be drilled to over-react and be too aggressive, but initiate the correct depth and angle to halt the option game.

STOPPING THE VEER

There are a few meaningful concepts that must be remembered in order for the triple option to be stopped effectively. The following are some of these ideas and thoughts:

1.   It is necessary that the defensive players know who is responsible for the quarterback, dive and pitch man on every defense employed.

This would include all stunts, slants and various maneuvers involved within the defense.

2. The defense must decide who is the most ineffective runner of all the three possibilities. If the pitch man is speedy, quick and a good threat at the corner, but the dive back (fullback or halfback according to the formation used) is not as strong, then more emphasis can be placed on the pitch man. Another example would be if the quarterback were strong, quick, shifty, etc., and more of a threat at the corner than the pitch man. The defense, therefore, must gear itself to this style of offensive threat and possibly defend it differently.

3. The defense should assign two men on the dive back. Since this man is going straight ahead versus the defense, he is bound to gain some yardage if only one man were responsible for him. However, if two defenders are in position to have him, the offense has to go to the corner.

4. It is important to have an attack defender maneuver from an outside-in approach at the dive back. This would signify that he would have to begin outside the nose of the offensive tackle since the quarterback is reading this area. Usually there is no offensive blocker employed on this defensive lineman.

OFFENSIVE PLAYS TO BE CONTROLLED

The defense must successfully attack the triple option first before it begins to stop the other plays in the series. It is necessary to control the dive back, the quarterback at the corner and the pitch man swinging wide. The offense can execute their sequence of plays with the same offensive action, but employ other blocking schemes also. For example, this would include utilizing one-on-one blocking principles. The diving back could receive the ball, or the quarterback could fake to him (using one-on-one blocking in order to get a block on the defenders aiming to stop the dive man) and option the defensive end. Counterplays must be halted also. This would include counterplays with the dive back countering away from the hole, the quarterback faking to the dive back and going away from flow or his faking to the dive man and handing off to another back driving up the middle away from the backfield action. The counteroption game must be controlled. This would include options that would occur after faking some type of counteraction. Other plays the defense must be prepared to defend are wide reverses, power from the triple option and play action passes from different offensive looks.

FORMATION DEFENSES

There are numerous coaches who believe certain formations will dictate the defense to be used. For example, if the Pro-type offensive formation (a wide flanker on one side and a split end on the other) were employed, the defense should utilize some type of four-spoke secondary. However, if the offense uses one wide-out (a Wishbone-T with a split end), an eight-man front should be used. This concept is considered important because a four-deep defensive secondary can cover the passing game versus two wide-outs and cover two offensive backs also. The eight-man front, therefore, can attack a three-man backfield more efficiently and still cover one split receiver. While these principles are good, many defensive teams have had success no matter what form of defensive scheme used.

IMPORTANCE OF CHANGE-UP

In order to attack the triple option game, it is very important that the defenses continually alter and change certain aspects of their defensive schemes. This should be done because a good offensive team will quickly adapt to the defensive keys being used versus them. For example, if the defense is pursuing well and experiencing success in defending the dive man and pitch back, the offense may attempt to utilize their quarterback more often and begin to counteract the pursuit of the defense. What the defense must accomplish is to change some defensive looks and execution of play to counterattack the offense. This would include defensive stunts, slants, maneuvers, etc. Different defenses and styles of play may help confuse the quarterback and the entire offensive team. To accomplish this, the defense must be well-drilled and prepared so a good defensive attack can be shown.

PRINCIPLES OF EXECUTION

When executing the defense versus any triple option offense, it is necessary to be well-prepared. Some coaches believe one method should be taught and used. Other coaches, however, think there should be numerous methods to attack the triple option, and these should be prepared when called upon. The following are a few principles and concepts utilized in defending the triple option threat:

1.   One defender on one offensive back — this is one method whereby one defensive man is responsible for a certain aspect of the triple option game. For example, a linebacker takes the dive back, the outside linebacker covers the quarterback and the defensive end is responsible for the pitch back. This is the easiest method, because each player knows exactly who he is responsible for and what his job is to defend his man. While this may be the simplest method, it may not be the best. However, a defense can go into a game with it, and if it does not work, use another principle.

2.   A second method is to have one defender responsible for one back but able to assist somewhere else also. An example of this would be a linebacker taking the dive back but being able to help on the quarterback; the defensive tackle covering the quarterback but staying alert for the dive back; the defensive end being responsible for the pitch man but remaining prepared to tackle the quarterback. This is a more difficult manner to attack the triple option, but it is a better attack versus it.

3.   Attack with different defensive maneuvers. This would include various defensive stunts, slants and angles that not only act as a change-up, but also may help confuse the offensive reading and style of play. Since the stunt is quick-attacking, the offensive must react fast to what is being executed.

4.   The defense must aim to stop the triple option with the front attacking force first. This would include only defensive linemen and linebackers.

5.   The defensive secondary should only be used for added support if possible. This cannot always be accomplished, since some defenses require secondary personnel to be utilized in stopping the triple option. However, if one of the offensive backs can get a one-on-one situation with a defensive back, the ball-carrier has an excellent opportunity to break one for a long gain. Therefore, if the secondary is used for support purposes only, it may have better results versus the triple option threat.

DEFENSES TO STOP THE TRIPLE OPTION

There are many defenses that can be utilized in attacking the triple option. The Wide-Tackle 6 is one example. Diagram 9-2 illustrates the Wide-6's ability to halt the dive with two men (guard and tackle), while the linebacker scrapes for the quarterback and the defensive end is prepared for the pitch man. These linebackers are in position to stop any countergame in the middle and are able to cover the quick pass to the tight end also.

The Tandem 4-4 is shown in Diagram 9-3. This defense is good because a great deal of stunting can be accomplished and the offense must be prepared for different defenders to option against. It is an attacking defense and can create confusion in the offensive backfield also. The tackle and inside linebacker stunt for the dive man, while the defensive end "plays" with the quarterback and the linebacker covers the pitch man. The responsibilities of the end and outside linebacker can easily be switched also.

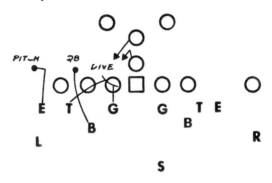

Diagram 9-2

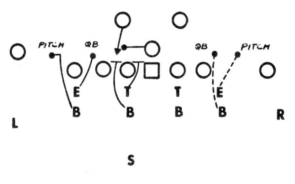

Diagram 9-3

Another defense that can be utilized is the Eagle-4 (Diagram 9-4). A four-spoke secondary is used for both the passing and option game versus the two wide-outs. In this case, the defensive linebacker and tackle control the dive back, while the middle linebacker moves up for the quarterback and the defensive end is responsible for the pitch man. A second method is to have the linebacker and tackle take the dive man once again, while the defensive end is assigned to the quarterback and the rotating defensive halfback covers the pitch back. The middle linebacker can assist anywhere along the line of scrimmage.

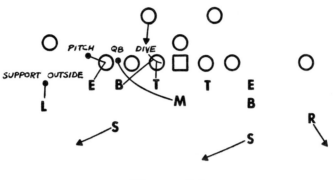

Diagram 9-4

Special defenses can be devised to meet the triple option threat. One example is indicated in Diagram 9-5. The defensive guard and tackle are directly involved in stopping the dive back. The left linebacker is in excellent position to halt both the quarterback (since he does not have to scrape far) and the quick pass to the tight end. The defensive end covers the pitch back. Toward the split end side, the defensive guard aligns in the center-guard gap and slants out into the offensive guard, while the defensive tackle slants down through the offensive tackle. The defensive linebacker can take the quarterback while the end covers the pitch. These roles can be switched, with the end on the quarterback and the linebacker taking the pitch back. Both linebackers, however, are in excellent position to stop the dive back and cover their responsibilities.

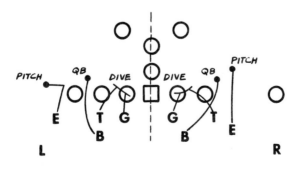

Diagram 9-5

ATTACKING THE TRIPLE OPTION WITH THE 5-4 DEFENSE

There are many varied methods the 5-4 Defense can employ to attack the triple option. Diagram 9-6 illustrates the defensive tackle crossing the line for the dive back, while the linebacker is responsible for the quarterback and the defensive end covers the pitch.

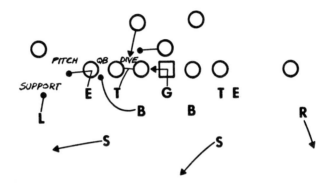

Diagram 9-6

A second method is for the defensive tackle to defend against the dive once again, while the end takes the quarterback and the linebacker covers the pitch man (Diagram 9-7). A third way is to have the tackle and end assigned to the dive and quarterback respectively, while the corner man rotates forward and watches the pitch. The linebacker slides along the line of scrimmage and backs up any of these defenders (Diagram 9-8). A fourth method (Diagram 9-9) illustrates the defensive tackle and linebacker on the dive back, the invert defensive halfback supporting quickly for the quarterback, while the defensive end protects against the pitch.

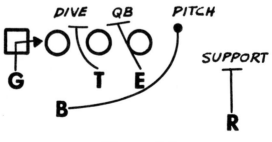

Diagram 9-7

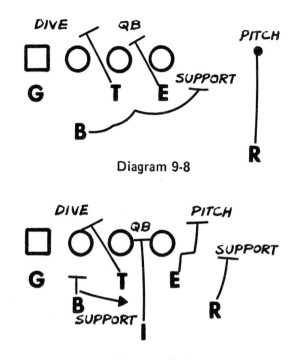

Diagram 9-8

Diagram 9-9

It is necessary with all of these defensive maneuvers that each position use good and proper steps for width and depth. The coach can assign one man to each potential ball-carrier, or he can utilize primary and secondary responsibilities along the line of scrimmage. For example, the defensive tackle and linebacker can be assigned to the dive back. The linebacker, however, can swing out if the dive man does not receive the football and assist on the quarterback. In this case, the defensive tackle should attempt to go hard and quick for the dive back so he may be able to upset the mesh between the quarterback and the dive man. The defensive end should come across the line of scrimmage so he can help tackle the quarterback, but still be in good position to cover the pitch back. The corner man must come up quickly and be in good position to tackle the pitch man along with the defensive end.

Stunt on the Corner

Stunting on the corner can be an effective weapon. It may cause confusion for the offensive quarterback. It is an attacking force which must create quick decisions immediately and put immediate pressure in the offensive backfield. Diagram 9-10 indicates two quick, hard charges. In both cases, the defensive players must stunt hard and fast, and be aggressive in the backfield. At the same time, however, each defender must stay low and under control to attack whoever keeps the football.

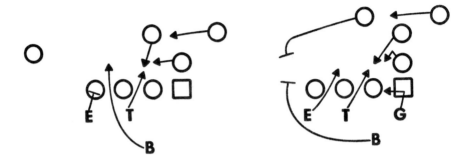

Diagram 9-10

Slanting Techniques

Another excellent maneuver along the line of scrimmage with the 5-4 Defense is the utilization of slanting by the line. As Diagram 9-11 illustrates, the left tackle and middle guard slant away from the formation while the right defensive tackle does not loop out. If the option came in the right tackle's direction and he was looping away from the dive man, good yardage could be gained by the dive back. Slanting can easily be utilized on the tendencies of the offense and certain field position situations. The middle guard is in good position if the option or counteroption comes in his direction also.

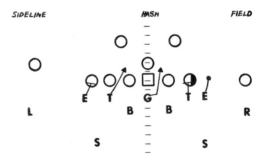

Diagram 9-11

Stacking from the 5-4

The 5-4 lends itself to different defensive alignments, because of the two linebackers and five defensive linemen. One example is the 5-4 Stack Defense. The defensive linemen can either wait and read, penetrate the gaps in which they are aligned or slant in one direction or another according to the strategy of the game (Diagram 9-12). In every instance, the triple option can be stopped if proper strategy is utilized along the line of scrimmage.

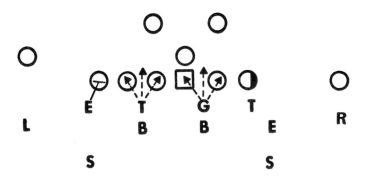

Diagram 9-12

ATTACKING THE TRIPLE OPTION WITH THE PRO-4 DEFENSE

The Pro-4 Defense can attack the triple option, using basically the same methods employed by the 5-4 Defense. Diagram 9-13 illustrates the Pro-4 Defense, with the defensive tackle and end securing the dive, the middle linebacker sliding for the quarterback, while the defensive outside linebacker attacks the pitch man. Another method is to have the tackle and end assigned to the dive, while the outside linebacker takes the quarterback and the middle linebacker covers the pitch man with assistance from the defensive secondary (Diagram 9-14). The third way is for the tackle and end to cover the dive back, the outside linebacker zeros in on the quarterback, while either the invert safety or defensive cornerback attacks the pitch (Diagram 9-15). The middle linebacker is free to slide along the line of scrimmage and assist wherever possible. The fourth method is for the tackle and end to be responsible for the dive, the invert safety covers the quarterback and the outside linebacker handles the pitch back. The middle linebacker is free again to help anywhere (Diagram 9-16).

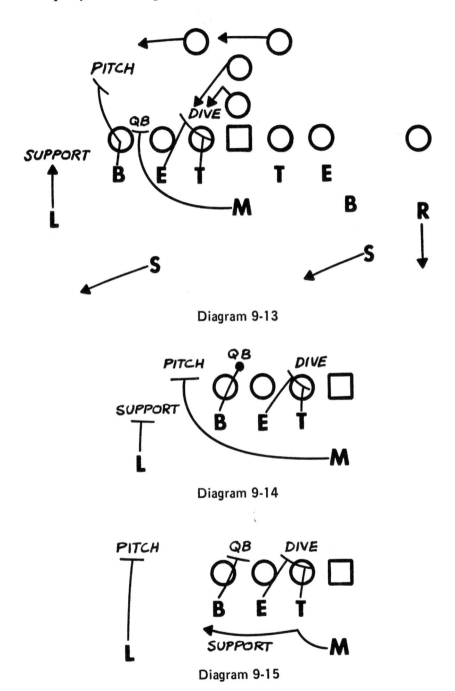

Diagram 9-13

Diagram 9-14

Diagram 9-15

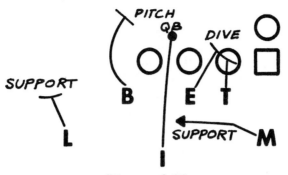

Diagram 9-16

Stunting and Slanting

Stunting and slanting from the Pro-4 can be employed to a certain extent. Stunting can easily be accomplished with the defensive tackle and middle linebacker stopping the dive back, so the defensive end can force the quarterback and the outside linebacker can cover the pitch man.

Slanting of the defensive line can be accomplished with simplicity and with some effectiveness. This should be done according to formation, field position, etc. Diagram 9-17 illustrates defensive slanting with both defensive tackles and one end. The middle linebacker can maneuver along the line of scrimmage for the option game.

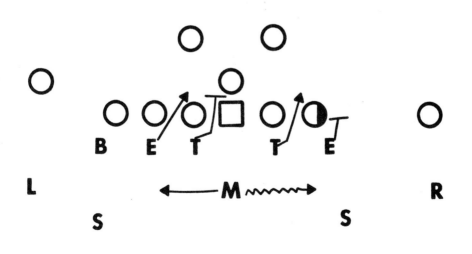

Diagram 9-17

ATTACKING THE TRIPLE OPTION WITH THE SPLIT-4
DEFENSE

The Split-4 defensive alignment is slightly different than the other defenses mentioned because of the eight-man front alignment. This is a good defense, especially versus one wide-out offensive set, unless a bad or inefficient passing game is utilized with two wide-outs. In attacking the triple option, the first order of business is to position one inside linebacker and defensive end to cover the quarterback and pitch man, respectively (Diagram 9-18).

Another effective method is to bring the outside linebacker down hard for the dive back while the inside linebacker maneuvers outside for the quarterback and the end covers the pitch back (Diagram 9-19). A third alternative is to again assign the defensive tackle and outside linebacker to stop the dive man, while the end takes the quarterback and both the inside linebacker and rotating defensive halfback become responsible for the pitch back. This is shown in Diagram 9-20. All three methods are effective and can be altered to meet various situations. In all cases, the away inside linebacker must step up to the offensive center and be aware of the counterplay and/or counteroption game.

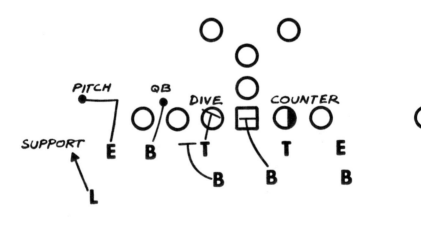

Diagram 9-18

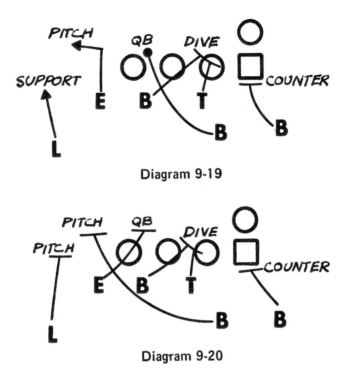

Diagram 9-19

Diagram 9-20

Stunting the Split-4 Defense

The defensive tackle and one inside linebacker could easily stunt, as indicated in Diagram 9-21, to halt the dive back initially. A good hard rush with this stunt can create pressure in the backfield quickly. Either the linebacker can scrape outside and the tackle maneuver inside, or the tackle can go out while the linebacker stunts inside.

Diagram 9-21

Corner stunts are effective as indicated in Diagram 9-22. Both the outside linebacker and defensive end can stunt hard and quick inside, or the end can squeeze down while the linebacker loops outside for the pitch back. Of course, middle stunts can easily be employed to attack any type of countergame in that area.

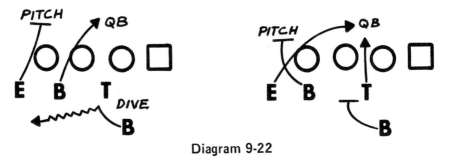

Diagram 9-22

Slanting with the Split-4 Defense

A slanting charge is effective versus the triple option, especially with field position and offensive tendencies. Diagram 9-23 illustrates a slant maneuver with the defensive line, while one inside linebacker stunts. The defensive left end stunts inside for the quarterback while the outside linebacker loops out for the pitch back. The left defensive tackle loops into the offensive tackle, anticipating the dive back, and can receive assistance from the left inside linebacker. The right defensive tackle slants to the inside looking for the counter-game, while the right inside linebacker stunts quickly for the dive back coming in his direction. The right defensive end slants to the left for any quarterback option, while the right outside linebacker is prepared for the pitch back. In every case, each defender goes aggressively to his area of responsibility, but remains low and under control, prepared for any offensive play that may develop.

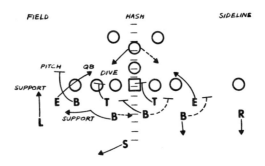

Diagram 9-23

DEFENSIVE SECONDARY COVERAGES

It is important with every defensive alignment used that the defensive secondary coverage be sound. Different coverages can be utilized including man-to-man, zones and combinations of each. The passing game of the triple option offense can be extremely effective, especially when offensive receivers are continually releasing from the line of scrimmage on every play. The quarterback can always pull up and try to pass the ball to any one of them. With this passing threat, the defense must have each receiver covered so the offense does not gain any amount of yardage through the air. For example, one simple pass from the offensive formation is the quick pass to the offensive end on the line of scrimmage (Diagram 9-24). Since the offense is using two wide-outs versus a three-deep defense, there are only two defenders that can stop the pass; i.e., the safety (man-to-man) or the outside linebacker. Since man-to-man is self-explanatory, the latter method is indicated in Diagram 9-25. In this situation, the inside linebacker and tackle cover the dive back while the outside linebacker backs off the line of scrimmage with the offensive end to halt the quick pass. The defensive end is responsible for the quarterback and the secondary levels to the flow, with the defensive halfback taking the pitch man. The outside linebacker, after the first few steps, can read run or pass and can easily come forward for any support on the quarterback or pitch.

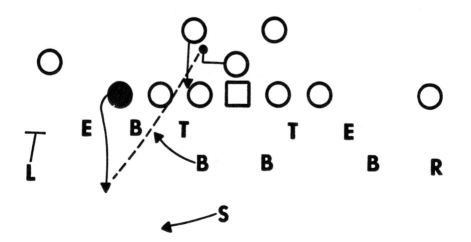

Diagram 9-24

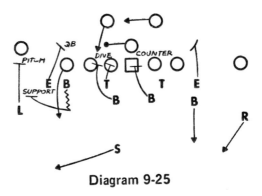

Diagram 9-25

The four-deep defensive secondary is in a better position to attack the passing game because of the extra defensive back. With a four spoke, at least one safety is aligned over the second inside receiver versus two wide-outs. Any coverage can be used, including invert, rotate or man-to-man.

ATTACKING THE OUTSIDE VEER

The outside triple option has similar principles and concepts that have already been mentioned; however, the play is executed one hole wider. The offense must practice this in order to become successful with it because various optioning points, techniques, etc. are different. The defense must be prepared also. Different defenders must concentrate on other types of offensive backfield play. For example, Diagram 9-26 illustrates the outside veer or triple option versus the 5-4 Defense. As can be seen, the defensive end must be alert for the dive back since the quarterback is keying him. The quarterback will then go outside and option the secondary contain man; i.e., the corner back or defensive invert (safety).

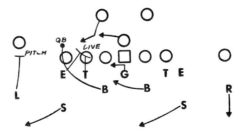

Diagram 9-26

In order to attack this play with success, the defensive end must halt the dive since the defensive tackle is being double-teamed. The inside linebacker can swing hard outside and cover the quarterback while the defensive secondary takes the pitch man. Good, hard, quick pursuit by the entire defense is important on this play. An effective maneuver versus the outside veer is to stunt at the corner in any available way so as to disrupt and place extra pressure in the offensive backfield.

OTHER FIELD SITUATION DEFENSES

A defensive team must be prepared to attack the triple option with the repertoire of defenses it has for the season. This includes different prevent defenses, short yardage defenses, goal line defenses, etc. The prevent defense must be fully prepared (Diagram 9-27), with each individual player knowing his responsibilities to stop the option. The same holds true with any short yardage defense.

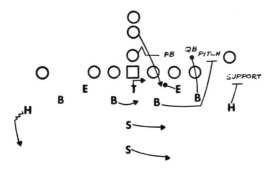

Diagram 9-27
A prevent defense attacking
the triple option.

The goal line defense is one aspect of defensive football that is often overlooked in attacking the triple option. It is very important that the defense be drilled against this offense if any type of success is to be achieved. The 6-5, the most often used defense on the goal line, is illustrated in Diagram 9-28.

In stopping the dive play, it is believed that three defenders should be in position to halt it. Since there are only a few feet necessary for the touchdown, and the dive back is driving straight ahead, it is important to stop the dive back first and then cover the

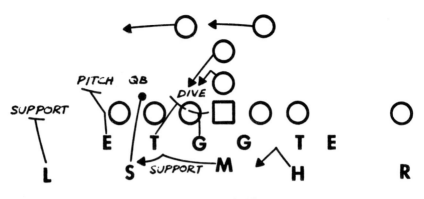

Diagram 9-28

other options. As can be seen, the defensive tackle, guard and middle linebacker converge on the dive man, while the defensive halfback and end cover the quarterback and the pitch man, respectively. This can easily be reversed so that the defensive end closes for the quarterback and the halfback widens for the pitch. The same methods can be employed, but with the middle linebacker supporting for all three options. He can be especially alert to the dive, but have the ability to slide outside quickly to assist with either the defensive halfback or end.

Stunting and slanting can easily be accomplished on the goal line with the 6-5 Defense. Again, it is important to attack in this way. Pressure and penetration is necessary on the goal line, and versus the triple option game it is even more important. Hitting the dive back quickly, possibly forcing the quarterback a little deeper, etc., is a necessity on the goal line.

Attacking
the Double Option

Attacking any double option of an offense is somewhat easier than with the triple option. For one thing, the defense has only to contend with two offensive backs carrying the football rather than three. Less practice time and drilling is necessary with this attack also. Basically, the quarterback will either fake into the line or come straight out at the defensive end. He will either keep the football and turn upfield for yardage or pitch to the trailing halfback. The defenders have only to worry about the faking back and whether he is to receive the football or not. The blocking schemes on the line of scrimmage are different also. Usually all defenders will be blocked in one form or another, except for the defensive men to be optioned.

The different options to be faced by the defense are many and varied. From game to game, different options may be seen and will have to be defensed, according to the type of offense utilized (a small amount of plays or multiple offense). The different double options to be defended during a season are the following:

1. The Swing Option.
2. The Split-T Option.
3. The Inside Belly Option.
4. The Outside Belly Option.
5. The Slant Option.

The Swing Option

This is a very popular option, because it is simple for the offense to install and execute. It attacks the defensive end versus all defenses; however, it could attack the defensive corner or halfback (safety) from the four-spoke secondary. The quarterback is instructed to come directly down the line of scrimmage and either keep or pitch the football according to the defensive maneuver of the option man (Diagram 10-1). The offensive wide-out and halfback block the defensive corner and outside forcing unit.

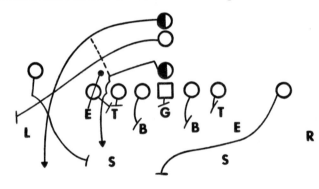

Diagram 10-1

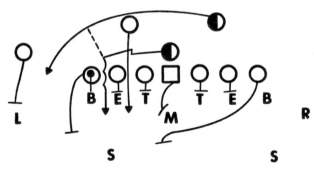

Diagram 10-2

The Split-T Option

The Split-T is similar to the swing option, except a dive back is used and a blocking back is eliminated (unless a three-back offense is employed). The blocking scheme on the line of scrimmage can change because of the fake in the backfield. As shown in Diagram 10-2, the defensive end is not double-teamed, because of the fake inside. The offensive end can now release downfield and have another responsibility.

The Inside Belly Option

The inside belly series is employed with a fullback aligned behind the quarterback. This running option can either go to the end in any defense or at a secondary defender in a four-spoke umbrella. The fullback fakes through the guard-tackle gap while the quarterback takes the ball out and options the defensive end (Diagram

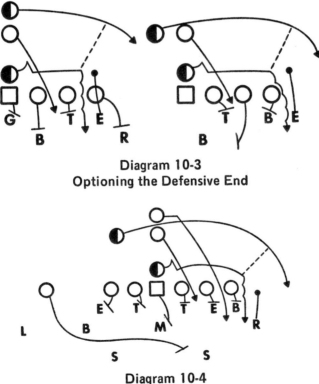

Diagram 10-3
Optioning the Defensive End

Diagram 10-4
Optioning the Cornerback

10-3). Diagram 10-4 illustrates another, but varied, inside belly series option. The quarterback first fakes to the fullback, next fakes to the tailback going off-tackle and then swings outside for the secondary contain man on the option.

The Outside Belly Series

The outside belly option will attack either the defensive end from an eight-man front alignment or the cornerback (or invert) in a nine-man front. The faking is different than the split-T and inside belly option. The fullback will fake at the off-tackle position, attempting to hold the defenders in this area. The quarterback will eventually take the ball "out of the stomach" of the fullback and attempt to go outside and option the contain man. Diagram 10-5 illustrates the outside belly option versus a nine-man front, with the quarterback optioning the invert safety.

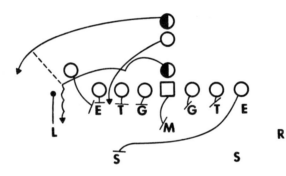

Diagram 10-5

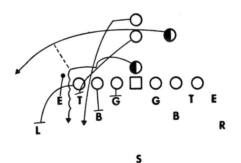

Diagram 10-6

The Slant Option

The slant option is similar to the outside belly option, insofar as the fake is being executed at the off-tackle position. In this case, the tailback slants off-tackle, with the quarterback faking to him. Again, the option is being executed on the defensive contain man, whether he be the end or cornerback (Diagram 10-6).

ATTACKING THE SWING OPTION

The Split-4 Defense

When combating the swing option, each defense can attack it with a number of different methods. It is important for each position to react and read properly, and execute techniques and fundamentals well. The Split-4 Defense (Diagram 10-7) illustrates the first method of attack. The inside and outside linebacker are responsible for the quarterback, while the defensive end covers the pitch back. The inside linebacker can assist on the pitch man once the quarterback releases the ball. The defensive halfback can do the same also. If the defensive outside linebacker is being blocked well by the offensive end, the defensive end can "play" with the quarterback while support is given by the inside and outside linebacker. The leveling defensive halfback assists the pitch man also.

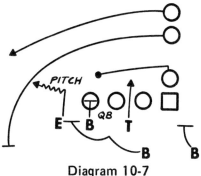

Diagram 10-7

If the offense is continually using the swing option and experiencing success, then stunting can easily be accomplished. Diagram 10-8 illustrates two methods. The outside linebacker can shoot hard for the quarterback while the defensive end covers the pitch. The second method is for the defensive end to slant for the quarterback while the outside linebacker is responsible for the pitch.

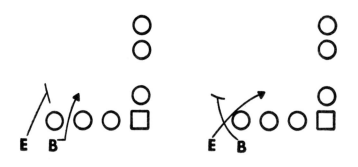

Diagram 10-8

The Pro-4 Defense

The Pro-4 Defense can stop the swing option by utilizing the up-front defenders first with secondary support. If this does not succeed, the four spoke would have to revolve on the pitch man. The first method of attack is to have the middle linebacker responsible for the quarterback as he comes down the line of scrimmage. If he is to be responsible for the quarterback, however, the defensive end must not let the offensive tackle and end double-team him and drive him off the line of scrimmage. If a double team is executed, the defensive end must "bury" himself so that the middle linebacker does not get cut off from the quarterback. The defensive outside linebacker can execute his initial steps, read the swing option and get into a position so he can cover the pitch without difficulty, and, at the same instant, tackle the quarterback if he turns upfield. The defensive secondary can be used as support on both the quarterback keep or pitch man (Diagram 10-9).

The second method of attack is to have the defensive outside linebacker assigned to the quarterback. The defensive halfback or safety, therefore, is responsible for the pitch man. The middle linebacker can now be used for support on either the quarterback or pitch back.

The 5-4 Defense

The attack methods utilized with the Pro-4 are very similar for the 5-4 Defense. With the first method, the inside linebacker scrapes off quickly in the off-tackle position for the quarterback. He must not be driven back by the double team on the defensive tackle or be cut off by a down block by the offensive end. Of course, if this blocking scheme is done, the defensive tackle is in excellent position to work his way outside. The inside linebacker is in better alignment to halt the quarterback than was the middle linebacker in the Pro-4. The defensive end is responsible for the pitch man.

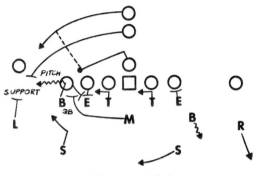

Diagram 10-9

The second method is to hold the defensive end accountable for the quarterback, while one of the revolving defensive secondary defenders is responsible for the pitch. The inside linebacker can help support either option man along the line of scrimmage.

Stunting on the corner is very helpful, especially if the defense is not experiencing success with this play. Diagram 10-10 illustrates a tackle-linebacker stunt, where the inside linebacker initiates quick pressure on the quarterback. The defensive end tackles the pitch back. The second stunt indicates a tackle, end and linebacker stunt. In this case, the ends stunt quickly for the quarterback while the linebacker swings out and is answerable for the pitch back. The third maneuver indicates a monster effect from the four deep. The Monster (corner) stunts down hard for the quarterback, and the defensive end loops out for the pitch back. The inside linebacker is in good position to assist anywhere along the line of scrimmage. If the

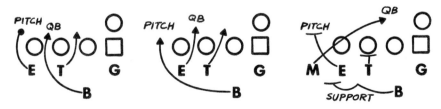

Diagram 10-10

defensive coach is disturbed by the threat on the off-side, the defensive line can easily slant or loop away from the Monster and both sides would be protected (Diagram 10-11).

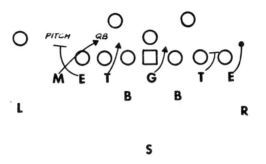

Diagram 10-11

ATTACKING THE SPLIT-T AND INSIDE BELLY OPTION

The Split-T and inside belly option are very similar in that a fake is being initiated inside to hold defenders in this area. The quarterback, then, maneuvers outside and options the defensive end. It must be remembered when a fake is made versus any defense, the offense loses a blocker. The defense, nevertheless, must respect the fake of the offensive back and may not be able to react outside quite as quickly.

The Split-4 Defense

The inside linebacker and the defensive tackle must first be accountable for the dive back. The outside linebacker is responsible for the quarterback, while the defensive end takes the pitch man. The inside linebacker can help support outside once he knows the faking back does not have the football. Another method is for the defensive tackle and outside linebacker to be assigned to the dive back while the defensive end takes the quarterback. The leveling defensive halfback attacks the pitch back, while the inside linebacker sweeps along the line of scrimmage, looking for the dive, quarterback and finally the pitch back. Any corner stunt can be executed (as was illustrated) versus the swing option; however, another stunt is indicated in Diagram 10-12. The defensive tackle stunts to the outside eye of the offensive tackle, looking quickly for the dive back. The inside linebacker scrapes outside for better support on any man

who carries the football. The away inside linebacker protects over
the offensive center for the countergame.

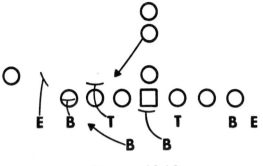

Diagram 10-12

The Pro-4 and 5-4 Defense

With the fake of the offensive back in the guard-tackle seam to
hold either the defensive tackle (5-4 Defense) or defensive end (Pro-4
Defense), it is best for the outside linebacker and defensive end, in
their respective defenses, to be responsible for the quarterback, while
the revolving cornerback should be accountable for the pitch man. In
either case, the inside or middle linebacker can help support along
the line of scrimmage (Diagram 10-13).

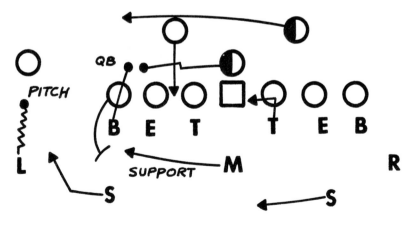

Diagram 10-13

Any corner stunts can be utilized from the two defenses to
confuse and place pressure on the optioning quarterback. Stunting

inside may be desired against the diving fullback or tailback. Slanting or looping of the defensive line may be another alternative, especially if the offense has certain tendencies or field position becomes a factor.

ATTACKING THE OUTSIDE BELLY AND SLANT OPTION GAME

The outside belly and slant option game can be a little more difficult to defend, because the offense is sending a faking ball-carrier toward the off-tackle position, with the quarterback optioning the defensive contain man. This would be a cornerback in a nine-man front and an end in an eight-man alignment.

The Pro-4 and 5-4 Defense

There will not be a double team at the off-tackle hole. Therefore, it is important for the defender stationed at that position to fight outside for the potential diving ball-carrier. This would be the defensive tackle in the 5-4 and the end in the Pro-4 Defense. The defensive end or outside linebacker positioned over the offensive end must fight the block of this man and should not close off-tackle too quickly, unless he knows the diving back has the football. If he is being double-teamed by a wingback, then both defensive secondary men (corner and safety) can converge on the option threat. If, however, the wing or flankerback release downfield to block, this gives the defensive end or outside linebacker the ability to get outside and cover the quarterback. The inside linebacker and middle linebacker from the 5-4 and Pro-4, respectively, must help support along the line. Diagrams 10-14 and 10-15 illustrate a flanker and wingback threat and the defense necessary to stop this type of option game.

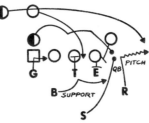

Diagram 10-14

The outside belly. Since there is a double team, the secondary reacts up quickly for the option, with support from the linebacker.

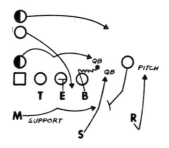

Diagram 10-15
The outside belly with a flanker. The outside linebacker must assist on the quarterback while the defensive safety must fight the block of the flanker. The corner revolves forward quickly for the pitch, while the middle linebacker supports.

Stunting can be an effective weapon versus this offensive play. Any defensive stunt that can hit the off-tackle position for the potential ball-carrier and have a defender protect outside is good. Slanting is another method. Secondary stunts at the corner area is a good method also. Another important factor is pursuit. Pursuit by the inside defenders away from the play is necessary because the threat is outside. They must support as quickly as possible to assist at the corner.

The Split-4 Defense

When this form of option threatens the corner of the Split-4 Defense, it is important that the defensive end does not close or

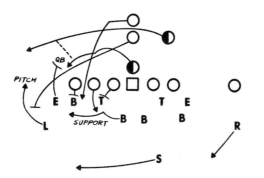

Diagram 10-16

quickly squeeze inside. The outside linebacker is responsible for the off-tackle hole. The defensive end should, once he sees the quarterback has the football, get under control and cover the quarterback. The defensive halfback must revolve forward, meet any blocker (in this case the fullback) and be accountable for the pitch back. The inside linebacker can scrape and either assist off-tackle or swing outside for the option (Diagram 10-16). Pursuit, again, is important. Any stunt can be utilized, either off-tackle or outside, to halt the play. Slanting of the line should be done also.

TECHNIQUE OF ATTACKING THE QUARTERBACK

When attacking any option by an offense, it is necessary that certain fundamentals and techniques be performed correctly. Techniques at times, are more important than the strategy utilized. It is usually a defensive end that a quarterback looks at on the option. This is done whether there is a fake inside or not.

When a defensive end faces an option quarterback, it is necessary for him to be completely under control. He should make his initial steps, execution and read the offensive play. Once the quarterback comes down the line, the defensive end should attempt to keep his outside foot back as far as possible. His inside leg is kept forward. He is in a good football position, with his shoulders square to the line of scrimmage, slightly bent at the waist and knees flexed. His head is turned in to the quarterback, with his hands out in front of him. The defensive end should try to squeeze down the line and close off any opening that may occur, because of splits and blocking schemes. This creates a smaller area for the quarterback to carry the football. Since he is responsible for the quarterback, he must tackle him immediately when he turns upfield. If he closes the hole, the defensive end will be in excellent position to tackle the quarterback. He should remain low and react quickly inside by pushing off his outside leg and foot and driving up and through the quarterback for the tackle.

If the quarterback, however, decides to pitch the football, the defensive end is in good position to assist the defender responsible for him. Once the pitch has been made, the defensive end will push off his inside foot and sprint to a cut-off point, where he knows he can tackle the ball-carrier. The placement of his feet has already stationed him to get outside easily. This may be straight down the line of scrimmage or there might be a slight angle to his pursuit (Diagram 10-17). With this technique, the defensive end is fully assigned to his designated man, the quarterback, and at the same time, he is assisting on the pitch. This technique can be used on any quarterback with all options, including the triple option threat.

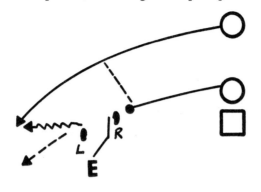

Diagram 10-17

TECHNIQUE IN ATTACKING THE PITCH MAN

When a defensive end is responsible for the pitch man, he can attack him in various ways. If he is not being blocked, the end can go directly to the pitch back and cover the path he takes. However, a better method is for the end to stay slightly on the line of scrimmage, be in good position to cover the pitch back — but be able to tackle the quarterback if he runs with the football upfield. The end accomplishes this as illustrated in Diagram 10-18. He automatically stations himself in an area that may assist the defender responsible for the quarterback. His stance and feet placement are the same as described previously, but without gaining depth into the backfield he can cover the pitch back and assist on the quarterback.

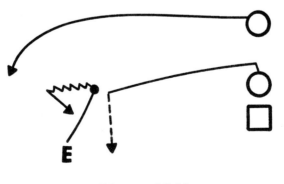

Diagram 10-18

If the cornerback, defensive end or outside linebacker is responsible for the pitch man, but is being blocked, it is necessary for this man to take on the blocker, keep his feet and body free of him and go for the pitch back. If the defender notices this type of play develop, he should immediately place himself in a good alignment to cover the pitch back. He should stay low, with the outside foot back, shoulders square and in a good football position to ward off the blocker. He may do this with either a forearm lift or the use of the hands if the blocker gets low. He must explode into the blocker and should not be driven back from the line or taken off his feet. A good deal of drilling and practice time is necessary to accomplish this. Drills of shedding the blocker and making one-on-one open-field tackles should be run through in order to respond properly to the pitch back.

Attacking
the Pro Strategical
Passing Game

The drop-back passing game is usually utilized at the college and high school level of competition. However, certain strategical techniques of reading and keying of the defensive linebackers and secondary are not done by the offense. In the professional leagues, and in a few colleges that execute this series, reading and keying is practiced diligently. In the former case, pass routes and patterns are designated with primary and secondary receivers. The quarterback drops back and scans to his first receiver. If he is not open on his cut, the quarterback looks to his secondary receiver. In the latter case,. however, each offensive man's move is dependent upon the direction of the defensive secondary and linebackers before and after the snap of the football. The quarterback reads the secondary before the snap. He then keys underneath coverage after the football is put into play. The receivers are keying the secondary defensive backs and linebackers for various coverages and maneuvers also. The offensive backs are taught to read linebackers and defensive secondary men. Each offensive man, including the quarterback, flanker, ends and backs, coordinate their play executed, to establish a better passing pattern according to what the defense has called and run.

DEFENSING THE PASSING GAME

Defensing the passing game requires a number of independent responsibilities on the part of the defenders in order to get the job accomplished. The following are what must be done for a defense to succeed against a good passing team.

1. A Good Pass Rush.
2. Good Linebacker Coverage.
3. Good Secondary Coverage.
4. Reaction to the Football.
5. Good Defensive Strategy.

A Good Pass Rush

A good rush can be the most important ingredient in a successful attack against the pass. If the quarterback has to throw the football any sooner than he desires, it can cause more incompletions and possible interceptions. Four defensive men are usually utilized to rush the passer, and seven defenders are employed in the secondary. Of course, more players can be used in the rush; however, there will be less men in the secondary for pass coverage.

Good Linebacker Coverage

Linebackers are usually not as quick or fast as offensive backs and wide receivers. However, they must be able to react properly to their respective zones or man-to-man coverage. Usually when man-to-man is used, there is either zone coverage deep or a rush is being established on the quarterback. If linebackers can help with underneath coverage, it greatly assists the secondary with their maneuvers. Linebackers must get their proper depth and width, break down in their areas and react to the receivers and football.

Good Secondary Coverage

The defensive secondary's role, in all coverages, is to stay between the receivers and the goalpost or play as deep as the receiver the defender is covering. Especially in zone coverage, each defender must get depth and width quickly and contain all receivers. If man-to-man coverage is used, the defenders should realize that there will be no assistance on their respective receivers. This coverage requires that secondary men cover all pass routes, including short and long patterns.

Reaction to the Football

Once the football is in the air, the defenders should react to it immediately. This includes all secondary, linebackers and even pass rushers. When the ball is thrown, anything can occur. If the pass is intercepted, the defenders have the opportunity to execute blocks for the interceptor. If the ball is tipped into the air, defenders reacting to the area have a good chance for an interception. If a fumble occurs, the defense has a better opportunity to recover it. If the pass is completed to an offensive receiver, the defense can tackle the ball-carrier immediately since everyone is reacting to the football. With every one of these opportunities possible, it is important that the entire defense be drilled in reacting and sprinting to the football once it is in the air.

Good Defensive Strategy

Strategy plays a very important role in the success or failure of good pass defense. Utilizing the proper coverage at the correct time is necessary. Offensive tendencies, formations, field position and down and distances can assist in good defensive planning for a particular game. Possibly knowing when and where a team will throw can be very helpful to the defense. Good strategy can take hours of hard work for the coaching staff, but it pays dividends in the long run.

READING THE PASSING GAME

Coaches throughout the country have always utilized some form of man-to-man, zone or a combination of each. However, when the offense uses the passing game, the defense usually tries to execute its coverage called. For example, if a zone defense has been called, there will be no change of the coverage until after the play has ended. The defensive halfback or linebacker goes to his designated zone and reacts to the football when it is thrown. A man-to-man defender covers his man, no matter which route executed. While it is important that all these defenses be employed, other defensive pass coverages must be installed to attack the pro passing game threat. If an offensive team does not read coverage on their drop-back game, the defense will be quite ahead in *playing the pattern run*, if defensive reading is done. With any type of zone coverage, it is better to *play the pattern* rather than go to the middle of the zone and get beaten. The coverages that will be discussed and explained in detail will illustrate how a defense can reverse the offensive process and "read" and "key" the pass routes employed by the offense. While the offense is attempting to read coverage, the defense tries to read the pattern and cover the receivers.

THE PRO PASSING GAME

While the defenses that will be illustrated can be employed against any offensive passing team, it is important for the coach to understand the philosophy and concepts of the pro passing game completely. Understanding helps to defense it with better methods.

The pro-type passing offense assumes it can "control" the movements of the defense. If the defense does one maneuver, the offense will do another. The offense, therefore, controls the football game or its defensive opponent. This type of offense believes that through alternate pass routes before and after the football, the percentages are in favor of the offense and a better pattern will be executed against the defensive secondary coverage. The quarterback will read the entire defense *before* the snap of the football. If there is a weakness, he may attempt to change the play on the line. The receivers and deep offensive backs are attempting to read the coverage also. Once the football is snapped and there has been no play change, the quarterback, backs and receivers are keying the defensive maneuvers for man-to-man or zone. Different pass routes can easily be altered as the receivers are on the run. The quarterback knows these breaks in each pass pattern executed and can easily pass the football to the open or more desirable receiver. Offensive backs stay in to block or release off the line according to what their linebacker responsibility does; i.e., rush or drop to their area.*

FORMATIONS EMPLOYED

The drop-back passing game usually presents one or two

*For a complete understanding of reading and keying principles of the drop-back passing game, consult *Winning Play Sequences in Modern Football* by Drew Tallman, published by Parker Publishing Company, Inc., West Nyack, New York: pp. 193-216.

wide-out receivers. Diagram 11-1 illustrates the most common formations; however, there can be many others, including two wide receivers to one side (twins), a flanker with no split ends, a three-man set to one side (trips), etc. In Diagram 11-1, the inside receiver is slightly split. This allows him room to release from the line quicker and gives him the ability to go inside or outside. Wide receivers are desired because they spread the defensive secondary over the width of the field and give the receiver an opportunity to maneuver on his patterns.

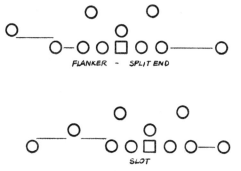

Diagram 11-1

In many cases, offensive formations can dictate the type of passing that will be used. For example, a split backfield can more easily release three men to the formation side than it could to the split end. However, if the fullback were stationed behind the quarterback with a halfback in his regular position, the offense has the ability to release three receivers to the split end easier than it could to the formation side. This is very important for the defense to realize and know. Scouting reports, game observation and films can play an important role in attacking the passing game. Game tendencies as to field position, down and distance, etc. are necessary also.

DISGUISING DEFENSES

In attacking the passing threat, the defense must have the ability to disguise its secondary and linebacker coverage. This can easily be done by moving defenders back and forth while the quarterback is barking his signals. Once he has finished, the defense can maneuver to the proper alignment it desires before the snap. To accomplish this, it is necessary for the defenders to move to their alignment and be absolutely prepared when the ball is hiked. One step out of alignment or not being physically prepared (stance for example), could hurt the defense's success. A three-deep defense (the Split-4) could easily disguise a man-to-man defense. The defensive safety shows this coverage for the quarterback and receivers, and at the last moment reverts back to zone before the offense has an opportunity to react.

UTILIZING THREE- AND FOUR-DEEP COVERAGES

The best coverage versus any passing team is the employment of a four-spoke secondary. This entails a seven-man front versus an offensive set, but four defensive backs are in position to cover five offensive receivers. Only one linebacker is necessary to assist in covering one offensive receiver. However, with the use of three-deep coverage, two linebackers are essential. This can put an extra burden on a defensive team, especially when man-to-man defense is needed. With rotational zone defensive coverage in the flat, it leaves only two deep defenders with the three-deep diamond secondary, but gives a four-spoke secondary three men deep for the pass. As can be seen, a four-spoke is more dependable long than the three-deep. This does not infer, however, that the three deep is not good versus the passing game. There have been many three-deep defenses that have done an excellent job against passing teams.

ATTACKING THE PRO PASSING GAME

Any type of secondary coverage can be utilized to attack the passing game. The rotational and invert zone from the three and four deep was described in detail in Chapter 6. These coverages can easily be employed and are very effective. Any form of man-to-man coverage can be utilized also. This can be accomplished from both the three- and four-deep secondary. While stunts can put more pressure on the quarterback, they are not necessarily needed. These coverages are basic to any defensive scheme and will not be explained further.

The Zone Pattern Defensive Coverage

Usually defenders are taught to drop and execute within their zone responsibility. However, defensing the offensive pattern is a strategy many coaches do not employ. For example, Diagram 11-2 illustrates a Pro-4 Defense with a four-spoke level coverage. One offensive pattern is illustrated. The flanker runs a curl while the second inside receiver (tight end) sprints to the flat. The near offensive back executes a hook route over the middle. In this case, the cornerback is keying on the inside receiver for the pattern to be employed by the offense. Since the inside receiver is doing an out route, the cornerback immediately "jumps" on him for coverage. The outside linebacker is reading the inside receiver also. Since the offensive right end went to the flat, he now can go directly to the curl area. Most offensive coaches try to complement their pass routes by running a receiver outside and putting another man inside. The offense attempts to widen the patterns, so the defense must spread to cover the routes. The outside linebacker realizes since the tight end went to the flat (outside), the outside receiver will most likely do some type of "in" maneuver (curl, square-in, hook, post, etc.). The outside linebacker sprints to curl and looks to the outside receiver for the route he is going to run. A curl has been executed, so he will cover the flanker.

The defensive safety is keying through the second inside receiver to the near back. He rotates to the deep outside third. Since the tight end went to the flat, he can be alert for an up pattern, but must be prepared for a post route by the flanker. He must be able to assist on both if the pattern is run and the ball is thrown.

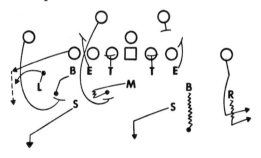

Diagram 11-2

The middle linebacker slides to the hook area. As he initiates his first steps, he is reading the movements of the near back and tight end. Since the tight end went to the flat, the middle linebacker can easily cover the offensive back. If possible, he should attempt to hit this man hard and knock him off his course. He now can play the hook receiver anywhere he attempts to go. The outside linebacker usually plays curl, but since the offensive halfback to his side stays in, he can cushion back through the middle and look for any crossing routes. He is responsible for the post pattern by the flanker. The right cornerback plays his deep outside third coverage also. Since there is only one receiver releasing, he can play this man tight (almost a man-to-man technique).

Diagram 11-3 illustrates the same defensive coverage, but a completely different pass pattern. Since the inside receiver sprints upfield, the cornerback will execute one of two movements. If no other receiver is threatening the flat area, the corner can retreat or cushion back with the flanker, so he can assist the rotating safety in the deep outside third for a long pass. If, however, he notices another receiver coming into the area (an offensive halfback in flare, screen, etc.), he must hold in his zone and play the offensive route the man initiates. On his first steps, the inside receiver comes off the line straight; therefore, the outside linebacker does not go directly to the curl area. He executes a tight man-to-man coverage on the tight end for any quick pass that may develop. Knocking the receiver off course during the pass route is necessary. The tight end can employ a number of patterns; i.e., out, flat, hook, square-in, post, etc. Since he does an out route, the linebacker covers him tough. If no other receivers are threatening his area (short), the outside linebacker can cushion with the tight end on a flag or post, or play the receiver hard on hook and square-in routes. The defensive strong safety rotates and must be prepared for anything deep. The away safety looks for the post as mentioned before.

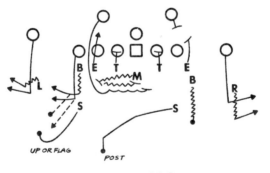

Diagram 11-3

Half-Zone and Half-Man Coverage

Playing half-man and half-zone coverage can be quite a challenge to any defensive team. It can become very complex at first glance, but once learned it can result in an excellent pass coverage and a good change-up for the defense. Zone coverage, in this case, is employed to the formation side, and man-to-man responsibilities are utilized to the weak side. This is a good field position defense, where man-to-man is used to the sideline area since the receivers have less area to maneuver. Man-to-man techniques must be learned and executed well. Since only four defenders are used on the rush with the following defense, man-to-man defenders must be able to cover their receivers anywhere they go.

Diagram 11-4 indicates half-coverage with the Split-4 Defense. However, any four-spoke defense can employ the coverage with probably greater simplicity than the three deep, because of the extra defensive halfback. The left halfback, safety and left outside linebacker execute zone coverage, but play some man-to-man within their respective areas. This is determined by the offensive pattern employed. The right halfback and right outside linebacker play complete man-to-man coverage. The inside linebackers will either play man-to-man or zone, according to where the deep offensive backs go.

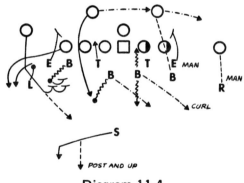

Diagram 11-4

The left halfback keys the inside receiver (tight end) for the vertical and horizontal movements he is going to perform. Since the tight end goes to the flat, he will cover this man. If the tight end goes upfield, then the halfback should cushion deep with the flanker, unless another receiver shows in the flat vicinity. The outside linebacker, to the formation side, is keying the inside receiver also. Since flat shows, he immediately looks to the wide receiver (flanker) and looks for his pattern. He will play this receiver man-to-man underneath as much as possible as shown in the diagram. The defensive safety attempts to key both the inside and outside receivers. Since the inside receiver goes to the flat, the safety should focus on the flanker and expect a post route. He should be aware of the up route of the tight end also. He must play both routes if they are executed. He will receive assistance from the level halfback and outside linebacker on underneath coverage. It must be remembered, however, that these defenders do not have to cushion deep with the receivers, especially if the offense has a good scrambling quarterback or different screens are finding success.

The inside linebacker to the formation side keys the near halfback to his side. He will cover the hook zone if the halfback releases to the zone side. However, if the near halfback sprints to the man area, he must play the back man-to-man. The right halfback covers the split end on a man-to-man basis. The outside linebacker, to the split end side, is responsible for his halfback man-to-man also. The right inside linebacker can be utilized for whatever the defense needs. If an extra rusher is desired, he could put pressure over the center. However, he can assist on zone coverage to the backside or cushion the middle area. He can play man-to-man with the outside linebacker on the halfback indicated and execute inside-outside, man-to-man coverage.

Another example of three-deep half-coverage and playing pass patterns is indicated in Diagram 11-5. In this situation, the same keys apply as mentioned previously; however, the left halfback does not rotate forward quickly, but hangs back because there is no threat in the flat. He can look for a square-out or curl by the flanker, or even a square-out route by the inside receiver. In this case, he is responsible for the flanker's pattern. The outside linebacker's man does not go to the flat, and therefore he will not look to curl, but will play this man tough off the ball. He can possibly cushion deep with the receiver on the flag route. The defensive safety is not sure what type of pattern will be executed, and therefore rotates and covers the tight end's flag route. The inside linebacker, again, goes to the hook area, notices the back swinging out and plays him aggressively until the ball is thrown. The other defenders play their respective men in the same manner described in Diagram 11-4.

Defensive stunts can easily be utilized with half-coverage for pressure against the quarterback. Since there are apparent weaknesses in the defensive secondary, the six-man rush must create a great deal of pressure in order to get the quarterback to release the ball sooner than he normally desires. Diagram 11-6 illustrates a middle stunt with the Split-4 Defense; zone is utilized to the formation side and man-to-man is employed away.

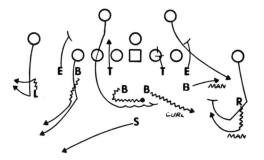

Diagram 11-5

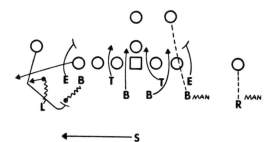

Diagram 11-6
Six-Man Pressure with Half-Coverage

Half-Coverage to the Weak Side

There are many instances versus a good passing team when zone coverage would be necessary to the weak side due to the formation tendencies, field position, personnel utilization, etc. Diagram 11-7

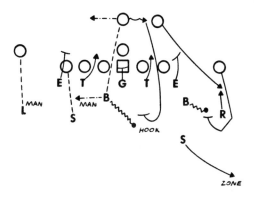

Diagram 11-7

illustrates this type of coverage from four deep with the 5-4 Defense. The Pro-4 or Split-4, or any variations, can easily be substituted instead. Similar keys and reads, as described to the formation side, hold true in this situation. Rotational coverage is employed to the weak side of the formation. In this case, the left corner and safety execute man-to-man principles with their respective receivers. A five-man rush is used. Of course, only four men are needed, and another defender could be dropped off into another area for extra support.

Switching from Zone to Man-to-Man After the Snap of the Football

Another form of reading offensive patterns is to change from a zone coverage to complete man-to-man after the snap of the football. Many coaches do not believe this can be accomplished, but it is being done. There are different methods that can be employed on the front and back side. The first example is illustrated in Diagram 11-8. In this coverage, the back side is utilizing complete zone coverage and

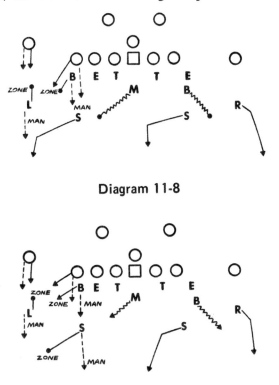

Diagram 11-8

Diagram 11-9

reading patterns. On the front side, however, the left cornerback and outside linebacker of the Pro-4 Defense key the inside receiver as was accomplished in half-coverage. However, if the inside receiver goes to the flat immediately, complete zone will be used. The corner will rotate forward, the strong-side safety will maneuver to his deep outside third and the outside linebacker will be responsible for the curl area. If the inside receiver releases straight ahead, though, the corner will execute man-to-man coverage on the flanker while the outside linebacker employs man-to-man on the inside receiver.

The outside linebacker does not have to be involved with this coverage. The strong-side safety and left defensive corner can use similar methods already described. When this is done, the outside and middle linebacker either play zone underneath or a blitz can be utilized on that side (Diagram 11-9).

When diverting from complete zone to man-to-man principles, a great deal is expected of the secondary defenders. To accomplish this strategy, the defenders should be aligned off the line of scrimmage (especially the deep men) a little more than usual. The cornerback can align at about 7 to 11 yards in depth compared to the 5 or 6 he is accustomed to. This gives him the opportunity to key the inside receiver and either pick up his receiver man-to-man or rotate quickly in the flat for zone coverage.

An Inside-Outside Technique

Another form of attack to the front side is the ability to use inside-outside principles on the offensive pass pattern. As shown in Diagram 11-8, the corner rotated forward and the outside linebacker went to the curl area, since the inside receiver sprinted to the flat. The corner and outside linebacker could easily execute man-to-man on their respective receivers; i.e., the cornerback covers the tight end while the outside linebacker is responsible for the outside receiver's route (curl, post, square-in, etc.). It should be noted that the defensive strong safety is rotating to the deep outside third and is in position to assist on anything long.

Utilizing Zone or Man-to-Man on the Weak Side

On the coverages already described, zone or complete man-to-man can be used on the weak or split end side. Zone, of course, has already been illustrated. Diagram 11-10 indicates keying and reading on the front side, while underneath man-to-man is used on the split end and offensive back away from the formation. The weakside safety can play half of the field and not rotate to the middle third. The strong-side safety should know this and not go to the deep outside third.

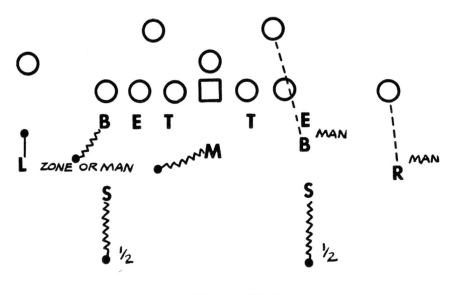

Diagram 11-10

THE TRIPLE OPTION AND THE DROP-BACK PASS

There are a few offensive teams throughout the nation that have employed the reading and keying of the drop-back passing game with the utilization of the triple option. The technique of keying and reading the defensive linemen, linebackers and secondary is accomplished almost entirely. Coaches believe that with this type of offense, they will outmaneuver, through complete strategy, the movements of the defense.

One fact must be kept in mind as far as defense is concerned. Since so much reading and keying is done after the snap, a great deal of mistakes can occur on the part of the offense; i.e., fumbles with the triple option and incompletions, or interceptions on the passing game. The offense needs a great quarterback also. He must be good enough to drop back and fire the football, and at the same time, have the ability to come down the line of scrimmage and option a defensive end.

Some defenses, including all stunts and maneuvers, are more effective against this type of offense. Man-to-man defense can be utilized. However, with receivers continually releasing from the line on both the passing and triple option, good run support cannot be realized at the corner against the option quarterback and pitch man. If man-to-man is used, good stunts must be employed to cover all aspects of the triple option with success. This can place a great deal of pressure on the quarterback as well as the passing game.

If the defense is going to play straight, then good zone coverage can be used. This helps not only for passing, but also gives the defenders the opportunity to "react-up" for the run quicker. Stunting should not be utilized since different zones will be given up on the field if the quarterback passes. Reading and keying of the receiver's releasing can easily be done with the passing attack as has been already mentioned. Switching from zone to man coverage against this offensive game can be highly successful also.

12

Attacking the Sprint-(Roll) Out Pass

The sprint-out pass with the numerous combinations and various styles can be one of the finest passing games for any offense. The sprint-out pass attempts to use one or two blocking backs on the defensive end with the hope that the quarterback can get outside the contain. It desires to exert pressure in one specific area of the defensive alignment. These areas would include the swing, short flat, medium outside, curl and deep outside areas. Any desirable amount of backs can release to these areas on sprint action. This would include one-, two- and three-man pass routes. All types of formations with their variations can be employed also. Different blocking schemes can be used versus the pass rush as well. The offense can utilize various throwback patterns also. Once, the defense starts to rotate and pursue quickly to the flow of the quarterback and backs, the offense desires to pull up and throw back. This can be done with usually one or two receivers; i.e., an end and back.

DEFENSIVE SECONDARY COVERAGES

Any defensive coverage can be used against the

sprint-out pass. Zones, man-to-man or various combinations of zone and man can easily be employed. If man-to-man is utilized, good support at the corner must be accomplished. If the quarterback can break containment, the secondary men are put under a lot of pressure to cover their respective receivers. The longer the quarterback has the chance to pass, the better opportunity he has to complete it.

With zone coverage, level or rotation should be employed toward the flow of the quarterback. This not only assists the passing game, but also can provide good support if the quarterback decides to run with the football. Reading and keying of the different patterns can be done with simplicity as was accomplished with the drop-back passing game (Chapter 11). The secondary and linebackers should focus their eyes on the initial movements of the receivers. This helps on the coverage desired so that the pass routes can be well-defended.

THE IMPORTANCE OF CONTAINMENT

Containing the quarterback may be difficult at instances because of the blocking schemes or personnel problems. However, if the defense cannot halt the quarterback's sprint route, not only is the defense in a bind, but the offense can use its sprint-out passing game to the fullest.

The Split-4 Defense has probably the best opportunity to contain the quarterback's route, because of the alignment of the defensive end. Diagram 12-1 illustrates the shading position of the defensive end and the ability to move him out slightly on passing situations. The Pro-4, however, cannot contain a sprint-out quarterback with the defensive end. The outside linebacker must contain, and if he does, certain secondary coverages cannot be employed or will be weakened (Diagram 12-2).

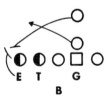

A Shade Position

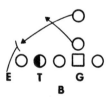

A Wider Alignment
Makes the Fullback's
Block More Difficult

Diagram 12-1

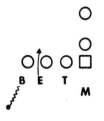

Difficult to Contain   **Certain Coverages**
                                    Cannot Be Employed

Diagram 12-2

Defensive adjustments can easily be made to counteract the contain problem. It should be stated, however, that when this is done, certain other defensive weaknesses may result. This is especially true on running downs (first and ten) when the offense has tendencies to run the football, but has the ability to pass also. Diagram 12-3 illustrates a simple 5-4 adjustment to an Eagle-5 Defense. The defensive tackle positions inside the offensive tackle while the inside linebacker aligns on the inside shoulder of the offensive end. This allows the defensive end, therefore, to move out slightly for better containment. As can be seen, the outside is well-contained. The Pro-4 can easily adjust also (Diagram 12-4). The defensive end aligns outside the offensive end, while the inside linebacker can maneuver either on the tackle or slightly wider. In both instances, the defensive ends are placed in a better alignment to meet any offensive blocker and contain the quarterback. At the same time, the linebackers can cover in the secondary with their pass responsibilities.

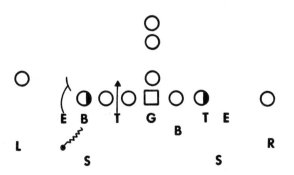

Diagram 12-3

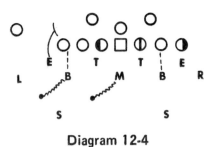

Diagram 12-4

Stunting at the Corner

Stunting at the corner, for the quarterback, can be a good defensive maneuver. However, the defensive end must be involved, and, if he has any responsibility inside, another defender must be used outside. With four-spoke secondary defenses, linebacker coverage can be lost. Man-to-man may have to be utilized. Diagram 12-5 indicates two stunts at the corner with the end and outside linebacker. Zone or man can be used because of the two linebackers positioned inside. The 5-4 Defense (Diagram 12-6) indicates different defensive stunts at the corner with the Eagle-5 Defense included. Man-to-man should be utilized. The Pro-4 and 4-3 Eagle are quite similar to the 5-4 and the Eagle-5 Defense and they will not be indicated. Slanting by the defensive lines can be a good attacking weapon, especially if employed to the open field or any offensive sprint-out tendencies. This not only allows good containment, but pursuit and coverage as well.

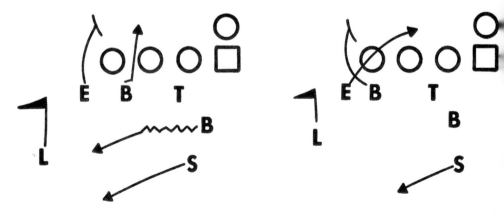

Diagram 12-5

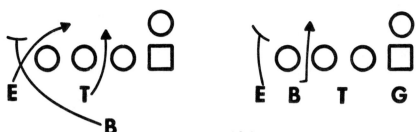

Diagram 12-6

ATTACKING THE THROWBACK

The throwback is an excellent variation of any sprint- or roll-out team. The offense hopes to force the defense to rotate toward flow so weaknesses will develop away. When this occurs, the quarterback will pull up behind the offensive tackle approximately 6 to 7 yards in depth and throw back to the back side. The defense must constantly work on this phase of the game. Some teams will rotate their defensive secondary (three and four deep) immediately on ball flow. If throwback is a good segment of the offensive threat, then the defenders should only level once the quarterback breaks the offensive tackle area. If this is done, rotation is not wasted to the flow of the quarterback, and the away defensive safety and halfback can assist on pass patterns easier.

An important aspect of any throwback is the ability of the defensive linebackers on underneath coverage. They must not flow quickly on the first movements of the quarterback. They should get to their areas of responsibility first before attempting to assist somewhere else. If man-to-man coverage is utilized, the linebackers should stay with their offensive receivers and employ good techniques. If there is a secondary defender playing a deep zone, the linebackers can then execute tougher techniques with their responsibilities.

Backfield action can assist the defense on the coverage to be used. For example, many offenses will send both backs to the sprint-out side (Diagram 12-7), which leaves only one receiver to throw back to. In this case, linebacker coverage can now move more to the flow instead of being concerned about the throwback. However, if one of the offensive backs flares away from the quarterback, the linebackers and secondary can adjust their coverage (Diagram 12-8). As can be seen, the right outside linebacker can cushion straight back if only one receiver is available. However, if a second receiver comes out of the backfield, he can go directly to curl or flat, depending upon the route of the receiver. The inside right linebacker can easily slide with both backs to a middle hook area, or possibly assist down the middle. If a back releases to the back side, however, he can now go to the backside hook and read the pattern of the two receivers. The diagrams illustrate the Split-4, but similar coverages can be utilized by any defense.

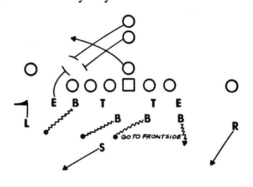

Diagram 12-7

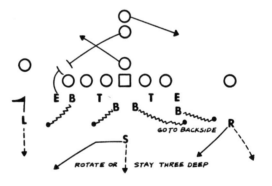

Diagram 12-8

DEFENSIVE END TECHNIQUES VERSUS SPRINT- OR ROLL-OUT

It is vitally important that the defensive end attempt to stop the quarterback's route and force him to pull up and throw the football. Once the defensive end reads sprint-out his way, he should immediately position low, keep his outside foot back and away from the blocker (usually fullback) and keep his shoulders square to the line of scrimmage. The defensive end must come across the line of scrimmage and squeeze down the blocker's path. This enables the end to meet the blocker quickly, puts additional pressure on the quarterback and gives the end the opportunity to maneuver outside if it is necessary (Diagram 12-9).

If the offensive blocker takes a hooking angle, this may force the end deeper, but he should not get as much depth as the quarterback. Gaining more depth as he maneuvers upfield gives the quarterback an option to turn up inside and break containment. This can put a great deal of pressure on the defensive secondary and its coverage (Diagram 12-10). If he steps slightly in front of the quarterback, he can halt this play by just stepping inside and making the tackle.

The defensive end should be quick, meet the blocker aggressively and get to the quarterback. As the blocker is about to make contact, the defensive end should step up with his inside forearm and foot, keep his outside arm and leg free and explode as hard as he can into him. If the blocker attempts to roll into his feet, the defensive end should use his hands and go around him. The blocker should never get to the end's feet, for if he does, all containment is lost and the quarterback has the opportunity to run or pass the football.

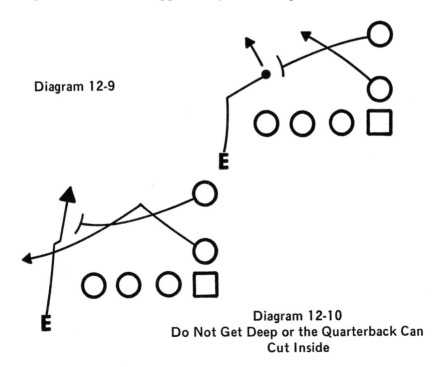

Diagram 12-9

Diagram 12-10
Do Not Get Deep or the Quarterback Can
Cut Inside

Attacking
at the Goal Line

Goal line defenses are usually called once the football is within 4 yards of the goal line. Some coaches do not utilize them until around the 2-yard line. Whatever the philosophy as to when and where goal line defenses should be used, it is important the defensive unit be totally prepared for any offensive formation and sequence of plays. Goal line defenses must be able to attack inside, off-tackle, outside and various passing games. Penetration by the defenders is necessary. The ball-carrier must be stopped immediately, and quick penetration into the offensive backfield has to be accomplished. Once pressure is achieved and established, then pursuit by the defenders should be initiated. Quick linebacker support is important also. Once flow of the backs and the play has developed, the linebackers must attack quickly and forcibly to the ball.

There are different defenses that can be used on the goal line. The most popular is the 6-5 Goal Line. Other defenses, however, include the Gap-8, 7-4 and their variations. Diagrams 13-1a through 13-1c illustrate these three defenses. The Gap-8 utilizes three "linebacker" defenders with the eight rushers, while the 7-4 uses four.

The 6-5 Goal Line attempts to execute pressure with six rushers and have five linebackers as support.

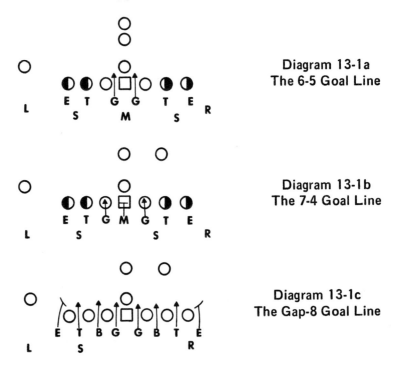

Diagram 13-1a
The 6-5 Goal Line

Diagram 13-1b
The 7-4 Goal Line

Diagram 13-1c
The Gap-8 Goal Line

ATTACKING WITH THE 6-5 GOAL LINE

Since the 6-5 Goal Line is the most popular employed defense, it will be explained in more detail. To attack any offense effectively with the 6-5 and its variations, it is important that a good segment of time be spent in practice on the formations and plays to be seen. The basic 6-5 Defense can be successful versus any defense and blocking maneuver. It is necessary, nevertheless, to have the ability to attack along different points of the line of scrimmage with various defensive schemes. The defense must have defensive maneuvers to attack the middle, off-tackle, outside and any passing patterns which develop.

Attacking the Middle

The defensive guards and middle linebacker (Diagram 13-2) are in excellent position on their alignment, initial movement and execution, to halt any play directly in the middle. The guards are aligned in the gap and shoot for penetration. Their first consideration is the quarterback sneak. The middle linebacker is in good position to assist also.

If there are inches for a touchdown (or even a short yardage situation upfield), the defensive guards can employ a pinch maneuver by driving their inside shoulders into the offensive center's knee (Diagram 13-3). Their responsibility is to drive the center back and possibly disrupt the ball exchange with the quarterback. The middle linebacker can easily scrape to either side on ball flow. A similar defensive stunt can be employed by the defensive tackles as well (Diagram 13-4). The defensive tackles stunt quickly for the guard-tackle gap and go for penetration. The middle linebacker, therefore, has good protection inside and can easily maneuver along the line of scrimmage. In this case, the defensive end can play normal. The middle linebacker has to be conscious of the off-tackle hole.

Slanting by the two defensive guards is another effective method in the middle. It creates defensive movement to certain formations and tendencies also. Both guards can slant together, or the entire line can be used. As shown in Diagram 13-5, the left defensive guard aligns in the center-guard gap. On the snap of the football, he will utilize a cross-over step with his inside foot and aim for a position upfield. The aiming point is the crotch of the offensive guard. He should go hard and aggressively through the offensive guard and not be driven back. Penetration is desired. This is not a loop technique where the angle is out first and up second. It is a direct slant to the area. The right defensive guard performs the same maneuver through the offensive center. He must be quick and aggressive also.

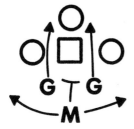

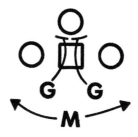

Diagram 13-2   Diagram 13-3

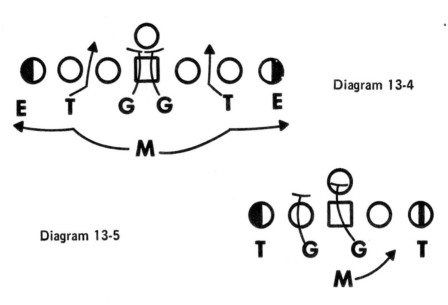

Diagram 13-4

Diagram 13-5

An out stunt is indicated in Diagram 13-6. This stunt is used only when the offense will not threaten inside. This is usually the case when there are more than 2 yards to go with fourth down or other situations, and/or tendencies that indicate the offense will not run inside. The two defensive guards employ their slant techniques through the middle of the offensive guard as was described. They desire penetration and then pursuit to the ball. The middle linebacker is concerned first with the middle area, and he then attacks outside quickly.

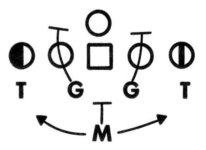

Diagram 13-6

The middle linebacker and both guards must practice the different blocking schemes that can be executed against them. Wedge blocking is popular, and these defenders must hold their ground. The defensive guards must be alert for down blocking by the offensive guards and reach techniques by the offensive center. The middle linebacker must be alert for blocks made by the offensive guards to cut off pursuit and isolation blocks executed by offensive backs (Diagram 13-7).

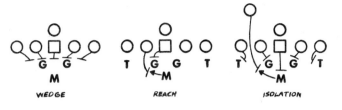

Diagram 13-7

Attacking Off-Tackle

Most offensive coaches desire to attack off-tackle on the goal line with power, although other plays can easily be used. The defense must attack this area if certain offensive tendencies exist. The defensive end can use a gap charge in the tackle-end seam if good support can be gained outside. This is usually done with the defensive halfback or cornerback (Diagram 13-8). The defensive tackle can maneuver inside also, as shown with a team stunt in Diagram 13-9. A good off-tackle and outside defensive maneuver is to slant the entire line outside (Diagram 13-10). The defensive tackle goes directly for the tackle-end gap and attempts to get penetration upfield. The defensive end scoots to the outside. He should utilize an open step and come directly upfield with the inside foot. It is highly desirable to have him squeeze this area inside so he can meet any offensive blocker trying to knock him out. The defensive guards should perform the same slant charge through the offensive guards as was explained previously. The middle linebacker can now slide along the line of scrimmage and help any lineman on the tackle. The out charge assists the middle linebacker to remain free from any blockers.

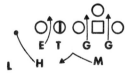

Diagram 13-8

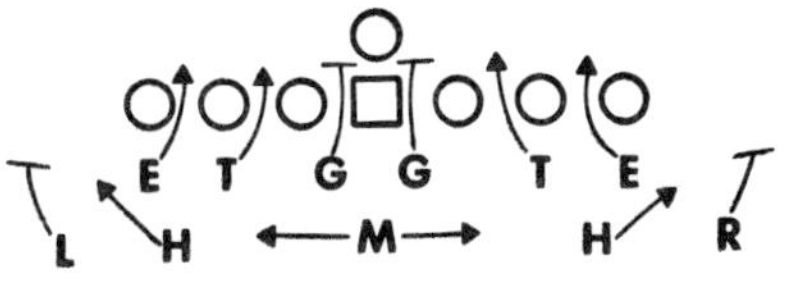

Diagram 13-9

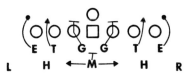

Diagram 13-10

Another excellent stunt for the off-tackle area is shown in Diagram 13-11, employing zone coverage. The defensive tackle uses a gap technique inside while the end loops out. The defensive halfback stunts the off-tackle area and meets any blocker coming his way. A similar stunt is shown in Diagram 13-12. The defensive tackle and halfback interchange their assignments. The defensive tackle slants outside while the halfback stunts the guard-tackle seam.

Slanting of the entire line in one direction only can easily be done. Scouting reports, films and possibly game observations will dictate when a slant charge should be used. The entire line, however, must first drive for penetration and then go on pursuit. Diagram 13-13 indicates a slant charge right or toward the offensive formation. The right end uses a loop technique outside while the tackle initiates a slant charge. The right defensive guard cheats slightly to a head-up position on the offensive guard and utilizes a slant technique in the guard-tackle seam. The left defensive guard explodes through the knee of the offensive center while the left tackle charges the left guard-tackle gap. The left defensive end goes "through the neck" of the offensive end. The middle linebacker's responsibility is the right center-guard gap and the left tackle-end seam. He has the ability to attack and support anywhere along the line of scrimmage.

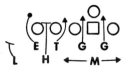

Diagram 13-11   Diagram 13-12

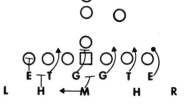

Diagram 13-13

Attacking the Outside

Many of the stunting and slanting charges of the defense shown in attacking the off-tackle area can be used for the outside game. The outside slant charge of the entire line as shown in Diagram 11-10 is an example. The slant charge of the line left or right is good to the side of the slant. The away defensive end, halfback and corner are not in the best position outside, especially when the defensive tackle slants inside.

A good defensive outside stunt can be utilized with the cornerback as shown in Diagram 13-14. The defensive guard drives hard in his aligned gap. The middle linebacker stunts through the guard-tackle seam, while the tackle shoots the tackle-end hole. The defensive end charges outside the offensive end while the cornerback stunts outside of him. The defensive halfback hits the offensive receiver so he cannot release easily on any pass situation. This is a good rush, not only for the outside running game, but for passing as well.

If a split end situation occurs on the goal line, then stunts can be utilized between the tackle, end and/or halfback. Diagram 13-15a illustrates the defensive end slanting inside for any running or passing play while the tackle loops outside for containment. Diagram 13-15b, however, indicates the tackle and end slanting inside while the defensive halfback (or linebacker) loops outside on flow.

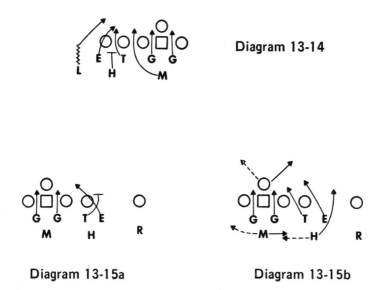

Diagram 13-14

Diagram 13-15a   Diagram 13-15b

DEFENSIVE PASS COVERAGE FROM THE GOAL LINE 6-5

Some coaches only utilize man-to-man on the goal line while others use zone. However, to have the ability to attack all formations, plays and pass patterns, it is necessary to execute both man-to-man and zone. Man-to-man coverage is rather simple and usually can be used by linebackers, because the offensive receivers cannot go deep with their pass routes. Actually, the defenders can cover their responsibilities underneath. If the pass is thrown over them, it must be a perfect one or the receiver and ball will go out-of-bounds (Diagram 13-16).

Zone coverage is good also. However, since it is on the goal line, the defenders should not go to a zone and try to cover it. This can put a tremendous burden on the defensive secondary coverage. If a quarterback can throw the ball accurately, he will usually complete it unless a defender is covering him well. Therefore, the zone coverage used should "play the pattern executed." For example, if rotational coverage is employed versus a wide flank, and a pass route is executed as shown in Diagram 13-17, the cornerback will cover the tight end and stay with him should he turn upfield. The defensive halfback will cover the deep outside quarter of the field, but since the outside receiver (flanker) runs a curl route, the defensive halfback will cover it. If the curl were a post, the halfback could assist on the route, with the middle linebacker running to his quarter of the field. Four deep is used on the goal line whether it be rotation or invert, with the cornerback covering the flat.

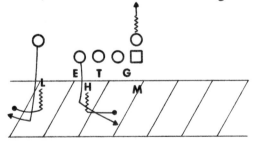

Diagram 13-16

A simple method to execute zone defense and not rotate or invert is to have each defender play one-fifth of the field. This can be used on both sprint-out and drop-back passes. The defensive corners, halfbacks and middle linebacker simply sprint back and play the defenders as they run their pass routes. If the receivers near the end line, the secondary will execute underneath coverage (Diagram 13-18).

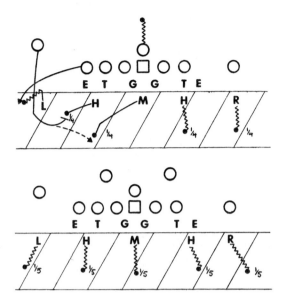

Diagram 13-17

Diagram 13-18

ATTACKING WITH THE GAP-8

The Gap-8 Defense cannot stunt as much as the 6-5, because there are eight defensive linemen attempting to penetrate across the line of scrimmage. However, slanting can be utilized to combat different formations, field position (hash-mark tendencies) and down-and-distance situations.

The Gap-8 is basically a penetrating defense. The defensive linemen must drive across the neutral zone in order to halt the ball-carrier for no gain or a possible loss. Since there are no real linebackers, each defensive rusher must perform his responsibilities extremely well, for if there is a breakdown in assignment, there is no defender behind the linemen to assist on the tackle. In many instances, the defensive linemen will not be able to drive through their respective gaps because of the blocks executed on them (down or reach blocks). However, the defensive linemen must not let the offensive blockers drive them off the line of scrimmage. They must hold their ground, keep leverage on their offensive opponent and pursue to the football.

An inside pinch charge and outside slant is illustrated in Diagrams 13-19a and 13-19b. The defensive linemen on the pinch charge shoot across the line of scrimmage through the outside knee of their respective offensive linemen inside. With the out charge, the linemen are going through the inside leg of their opponent. In both instances, the defense is attempting to gain penetration by pushing the offensive linemen back off the line of scrimmage. Once contact and penetration has been established, the linemen try to get on a pursuit course that will take them to the ball-carrier.

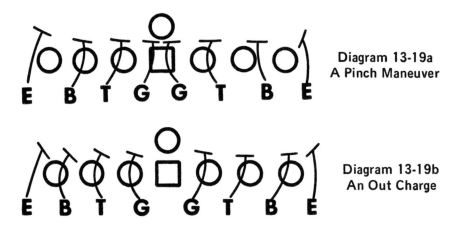

Diagram 13-19a
A Pinch Maneuver

Diagram 13-19b
An Out Charge

Slant movements of the defensive line can easily be utilized by using a combination of the pinch and out charge. Diagram 13-20 illustrates a slant maneuver left. The left side of the line employs an out charge and the right side uses a pinch technique. These should only be used with tendency situations.

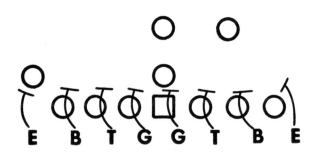

Diagram 13-20

PASS COVERAGE WITH THE GAP-8 DEFENSE

Since there are only three deep defenders in the secondary, the best coverage is man-to-man. If the offense splits an end, the defensive end or linebacker can easily back off the line and use man-to-man coverage techniques. Zone can be difficult with three or four men in the coverage. Man-to-man coverage is shown in Diagram 13-21. The defensive ends must be responsible for the third man out of the backfield if he should release.

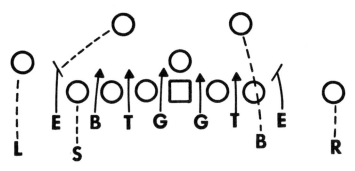

Diagram 13-21
Man-to-Man Coverage

COMBINATION OF 6-5 AND GAP-8

There can be certain strategical instances when the defense would want to employ a combination of both the 6-5 and the Gap-8 Defense. This can easily be accomplished. Versus two tight ends, only seven linemen are necessary, with a middle linebacker in excellent position to flow along the line of scrimmage. Diagram 13-22 illustrates a 6-5 look on the left (toward the formation) and a Gap-8 look off-side. With this defense, the middle linebacker can flow to the Gap-8 side easily and assist on any running play. He executes his normal responsibilities to the 6-5 side. Slanting maneuvers can easily be utilized on either side and stunting can remain a part of the strategy toward the 6-5 look.

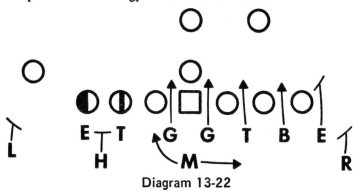

Diagram 13-22

Index

A

Alignment of defense, 18
Angling defensive line, 84-85
Angling lines, attacking off-tackle and out-
side with, 111-113
Attacking offenses, 18-23
(see also "Offenses, attacking")

B

Balanced offensive formations, 49
Bootleg, defensing, 103

C

Change-up, importance of in attacking triple
option, 170
Closed offensive formations, 48
Containment of quarterback, importance of,
218-220
stunting at corner, 220
"Counter off-tackle" game, playing, 101-102
Countergame, defensing, 75-76
Crackback block, defensing, 103
Cross-block, defensing, 98

D

Deep areas, attacking, 154-166
disguising defenses, 158
five rotate or invert coverage, 164
four-deep zone coverage, 160
four-one prevent zone, 163-164
long pass, attacking, 156-157
man-to-man defenses, 160
man-to-man with free safety,
utilizing, 160-162
pressure, attacking with, 165-166
secondary play, 157-158
three-deep versus four-deep secondary,
159-160

Deep areas, attacking *(continued)*
three-man defensive rushes, 164-165
three-one prevent zone, 162-163
two-deep zone, employing, 159
Defense that attacks offense, fielding, 15-26
attacking offenses, 18-23
alignment, 18
all areas, attacking, 22
all defensive adjustments, need
for, 21-22
angles, 19-20
defense as fun, 23
football knowledge and intelligence, 21
jumping of defenses, 21
keys, reads and coaching
points, proper, 19
personnel and defenses, 22-23
strategy, proper, 22
stunts, individual and team, 19
teaching, successful, importance
of, 23
techniques, fundamentals and
execution, proper, 18-19
coach's utilization of defenses, 15-16
defensive caller, coach and, 24
eight-and-nine-man defensive fronts,
16-17
maneuvers, strategic defensive, 25-26
no offense is perfect, 24-25
purpose, 24
scouting, importance of, 25
Defenses, attacking, eight most widely used,
27-46
5-4 Oklahoma defense, 38-39
cornerbacks and safeties, 39
end, 39
linebackers, 38-39
middle guard, 38
strengths and weaknesses of,
42
tackles, 39
other, 43-46
Eagle-5 Odd-Box-Corner

Defenses, attacking (*continued*)
        defense, 43-44
        5-3-3 in Odd-Diamond defense,
          43
        Gap-8 Even Goal Line defense,
          46
        6-5 Even-Box Goal Line
          defense, 45
        Wide-Tackle 6 Even-Diamond
          defense, 44-45
    Pro 4-3 defense, 33-37
        cornerbacks, 37
        end, 36
        middle linebacker, 35
        outside linebacker, 36-37
        safeties, 37
        strengths and weaknesses of,
          41-42
        tackles, 35-36
    Split-4 defense, executing, 28-33
        ends, 32
        halfbacks, 32-33
        inside linebackers, 28-30
        outside linebackers, 31
        purpose of, 28
        safety, 33
        strengths and weaknesses of,
          40-41
        tackles, 30-31
    strengths and weaknesses of each,
        40-42
Defenses, coach's utilization of, 15-16
Defensive caller, coach and, 24
Disguising defensive coverages, 128-129
    in deep areas, 158
Double-lead isolation play, playing against,
    73-74
Double option, attacking, 187-200
    different, 187-188
    inside belly option, 189-190
    outside belly series, 190
    outside belly and slant option game,
        attacking, 196-198
        Pro-4 and 5-4 defense, 196-197
        Split-4 defense, 197-198
    pitch man, technique of attacking,
        199-200
    quarterback, technique of attacking,
        198-199
    slant option, 191
    Split-T option, 189
    Split-T and inside belly option,
        attacking, 194-196
        Pro-4 and 5-4 defense, 195-196
        Split-4 defense, 194-195
    swing option, 188
    swing option, attacking, 191-194
        5-4 defense, 192-194
        Pro-4 defense, 192
        Split-4 defense, 191

Double-team block, defensing, 96-97
Double Wing formation, strengths, weak-
    nesses and series of, 64-65
Double Wing "T" formation, strengths, weak-
    nesses and series of, 59-60
Draw play, attacking, 76-77

E

Eagle-4 to stop triple option, 173-174
Eagle-5 Odd-Box-Corner defense, 43-44
Eight-and-nine-man defensive fronts, 16-17

F

Five-deep secondary attack, 164
5-3-3 in Odd Diamond defense, 43
5-4 defense, using to attack triple option,
    174-177
    slanting techniques, 176
    stacking from, 177
    stunt on corner, 175-176
5-4 Oklahoma defense, 38-39
    cornerbacks and safeties, 39
    end, 39
    linebackers, 38-39
    middle guard, 38
    strengths and weaknesses oı, 4
    tackles, 39
5-4 Oklahoma stunt, 80-82
Five rotate, utilizing in deep areas, 164
Flanker or slot, defensive coverage of before
    offensive snap, 120-125
    front alignment, bringing defender
        from, 125
    new defense, installing, 120
    pre-rotating secondary, 121-125
Flat, different defensive coverages in,
    121-125
Flat areas, attacking, 115-138 (see also
    "Wide-outs and flats, attacking")
Fold block, defensing, 100
Fold maneuver, defensing, 74-75
Four-deep secondary, using to attack flat,
    129-131
    to halt passing situation, 115-116, 117
Four-one prevent zone, attacking with,
    163-164
Fun, defense as, 23

G

Gap-8, attacking with, 233-234
Gap-8 Even Goal Line defense, 46
Goal line, attacking, 225-235
    defenses, different, 225-226
    Gap-8, attacking with, 233-234

Goal line, attacking *(continued)*
    pass coverage with Gap-8 defense,
        234-235
    pass coverage from goal line 6-5,
        defensive, 232
    6-5 and Gap-8, combination of, 235
    6-5 goal line, attacking with, 226-231
        middle, attacking, 226-229
        off-tackle, attacking, 229-230
        outside, 231

H

Hook areas, attacking, 139-153 (see also
    "Inside receivers and hook areas,
        attacking")
Hook block, defensing, 102

I

Inside belly option, 189-190
Inside belly option, attacking, 194-196
    (see also "Split-T and inside belly
        option. . . .")
Inside receivers and hook areas, attacking,
    139-153
    inside game, defenders for, 144-145
    inside receivers, covering with special
        defenses, 152-153
    inside receivers coming off line of
        scrimmage, attacking, 143-144
    linebacker coverage, 142-143
    man-to-man coverage, 149-150
    man-to-man with free safety coverage,
        151
    man-to-man with underneath zone
        coverage, 152
    varied inside receivers, 140-142
    zone coverage, utilizing, 146-148
Inside reverse game, playing, 101-102
    stopping, 76
Intelligence about football essential for
    coach, 21
Invert coverage, utilizing in deep areas, 164
    in three-deep rotation, 132
Invert coverage versus wide-out receivers,
    131
Isolation play, playing against, 72-74

J

Jumping of defenses, 21

K

Kick-out block, defensing, 98-100

K

Knowledge of football essential for coach,
    21

L

Linebacker coverage, 142-143
    essential for successful passing game,
        202
Long pass, attacking, 156-157
Looping lines, attacking off-tackle and out-
    side lines with, 111-113

M

Man-to-man coverage, 149-150
    with free safety coverage, 151
    with underneath zone coverage, 152
Maneuvers, strategic defensive, 25-26
Middle, attacking, 67-85
    alignments, others, using, 68-70
    angling, 84-85
    offensive maneuvers, defensing, 71-77
        countergame, defensing, 75-76
        draw play, attacking, 76-77
        fold maneuver, defensing,
            74-75
        inside reverse, stopping, 76
        isolation, playing against the,
            72-74
        other techniques, defensing, 77
        (see also "Offensive
            maneuvers, middle, de-
            fensing")
        trap, attacking, 71-72
    offensive maneuvers, preparedness
        for, 67-68
    stunts, attacking with, 77-83
        5-4 Oklahoma, 80-82
        Pro 4-3, 82-83
        Split-4, 78-80

N

Nine-man defensive front, 16-17

O

Off-tackle and outside, attacking, 87-113
    angling lines, using to attack off-tackle
        and outside, 111-113
    importance of, 87
    maneuvers, different, 88-89
        series of plays, offensive, 89
    off-tackle, attacking with other align-
        ments, 90-93
    off-tackle versus different offensive

Off-tackle and outside, attacking *(continued)*
    maneuvers, 96-102
      "counter off-tackle," 101-102
      cross-block, 98
      double-team block, 96-97
      fold block, 100
      inside reverse, 101-102
      kick-out block, 98-100
      one-on-one block, 96
      power game, 101
      step-around maneuver, 100
      trap, stopping, 101
  off-tackle and outside, attacking with
    angling lines, 111-113
  outside, attacking with other align-
    ments, 93-95
  outside, attacking with Split-4, 5-4,
    and Pro-4 defenses, 110-111
  outside versus different offensive
    maneuvers, 102-104
      bootleg, 103
      crackback block, 103
      hook block, 102
      quick pitch, 104
  Pro-4 defense, attacking off-tackle
    with, 108-109
  stunts, attacking off-tackle with,
    104-108
    5-4 defense, 106-108
    Split-4 defense, 104-106
Offenses, attacking, 18-23
  alignment, 18
  all areas, attacking, 22
  all defensive adjustments, need for,
    21-22
  angles, 19-20
  football knowledge and intelligence,
    21
  fun, defense, as, 23
  jumping of defenses, 21
  keys, reads and coaching points,
    proper, 19
  personnel and defenses, 22-23
  strategy, proper, 22
  stunts, individual and team, 19
  teaching, successful, importance of,
    22-23
  techniques, fundamentals and execu-
    tion, proper, 18-19
Offensive maneuvers, middle, defensing,
    71-77
  countergame, defensing, 75-76
  draw play, attacking, 76-77
  fold maneuver, defensing, 74-75
  inside reverse, stopping, 76
  isolation, playing against the, 72-74
  other techniques, defensing, 77
    one-on-one block, 77
    wedge block, 77
  trap, attacking, 71-72

Offensive sets, formations and maneuvers,
    strengths and weaknesses of,
    47-66
  classification of, 47-50
    balanced, 49
    closed, 48
    wide, 49-50
  strengths, weaknesses and series,
    57-66
    Double Wing, 64-65
    Double Wing "T" formation,
      59-60
    Pro Formation, 62-63
    Short Punt, 65-66
    Shotgun Formation, 66
    Single Wing, 63-64
    "T" formation, 58
    Tight Slot, 61
    Wide Slot—Split Backfield,
      61-62
    Wing "T" formation, 58-59
    Wing "T" Formation—Split
      End, 60-61
  variations of, 50-57
    in-the-backfield adjustments,
      54-57
    on-the-line adjustments, 51-54
One-on-one block, defensing, 77, 96
Outside, attacking, 87-113 (see also "Off-
    tackle and outside, attacking")
Outside belly game, attacking, 196-198
  Pro-4 and 5-4 defense, 196-197
  Split-4 defense, 197-198
Outside belly series, 190

                P

Pass, long, attacking, 156-157
Pass routes, offensive, attacking, 136-138
  flat route, covering, 136-137
  "in routes" from wide receiver, 138
  "out routes" by wide receiver, 138
  seam route, covering, 137
  swing route, covering, 137
Pass rush, good, essential for successful
    defense of passing game, 202
Passing game, how to attack, 154-166
  (see also "Deep areas, attacking")
Passing game, pro-strategical, attacking,
    201-215
  defensing, 202-203
  disguising defenses, 205-206
  formations employed, 204-205
  pro passing game, 204
  pro passing game, attacking, 206-214
    half-coverage to weak side,
      211-214
    half-zone and half-man coverage,
      208-211

Passing game, pro-strategical *(continued)*
    inside-outside technique, 213
    zone to man to-man after snap of football, switching from, 212-213
    zone or man-to-man on weak side, 213-214
    zone pattern defensive coverage, 206-208
  reading, 203-204
  three- and four-deep coverages, utilizing, 206
  triple option and drop-back pass, 214-215
Pitch man, technique of attacking, 199-200
Power game, defensing, 101
Pressure, attacking with, 165-166
Pro Formation, strengths, weaknesses and series of, 62-63
Pro-4 defense, attacking off-tackle with, 108-109
  attacking triple option with, 177-179
  stunting and slanting, 179
Pro 4-3 defense, executing, 33-37
  cornerbacks, 37
  end, 36
  middle linebacker, 35
  outside linebacker, 36-37
  safeties, 37
  strengths and weaknesses of, 41-42
  tackles, 35-36
Pro 4-3 stunts, 82-83
Pro Strategical passing game, attacking, 201-215 (see also "Passing game, pro-strategical . . .")
Purpose of defense, 24

Q

Quarterback, technique of attacking, 198-199
Quick pitch, defensing, 104

R

Reading passing game, 203-204
Receiver, wide-out, attacking with three- and four-deep secondaries, 133-136
  all zone coverage with one defender playing man-to-man, 136
  man underneath coverage with deep zone, 134
  one-on-one, man-to-man coverage, 134
  two man-to-man defenders, 135
  zone underneath coverage with deep man-to-man, 134-135
Rotational coverage versus wide-out situation, 130

S

Scouting, importance of, 25
Secondary coverage, good, essential for successful defense of passing game, 202-203
Short Punt, strengths, weaknesses and series of, 65-66
Shotgun Formation, strengths, weaknesses and series of, 66
Single Wing formation, strengths, weaknesses and series of, 63-64
6-5 Even-Box Goal Line defense, 45
6-5 goal line, attacking with, 226-231
  middle, attacking, 226-229
    out stunt, 228
  off-tackle, attacking, 229-230
  outside, attacking, 231
Slant and loop, 84-85
  attacking off-tackle and outside with, 111-113
Slant option game, attacking, 196-198
  Pro-4 and 5-4 defense, 196-197
  Split-4 defense, 197-198
Slanting with Split-4 defense, 182
Split end, defensive coverage of before offensive snap, 126-128
  front alignment, bringing defender from, 126
  new defense, installing, 127
  pre-rotating secondary, 127-128
Split-4 defense, attacking triple option with, 180-182
  slanting, 182
  stunting, 181-182
Split-4 defense, executing, 28-33
  ends, 32
  halfbacks, 32-33
  inside linebackers, 28-30
  outside linebackers, 31
  purpose of, 28
  safety, 33
  strengths and weaknesses of, 40-41
  tackles, 30-31
Split-4 stunt, 78-80
Split-T option, 189
Split-T and inside belly option, attacking, 194-196
  Pro-4 and 5-4 defense, 195-196
  Split-4 defense, 194-195
Sprint-(Roll) out pass, attacking, 217-223
  containment, importance of, 218-220
    stunting at corner, 220
  defensive end techniques versus sprint- or roll-out, 222-223
  secondary coverages, defensive, 217-218
  throwback, attacking, 221-222

Step-around maneuver, defensing, 100
Strategy, good defensive, essential for suc-
    cessful defense of passing game, 203
Strategy, proper, essential for coach's de-
    fense, 22
Stunts, attacking middle with, 77-83
    5-4 Oklahoma, 80-82
    Pro 4-3, 82-83
    Split-4, 78-80
Stunts, individual and team, on defense, 19
Stunts, using to attack off-tackle, 104-108
    (see also "Off-tackle and outside,
        attacking")
Swing option, 188
    attacking, 191-194
        5-4 defense, 192-194
        Pro-4 defense, 192
        Split-4 defense, 191

                        T

"T" formation, strengths, weaknesses and
    series of, 58
Tandem 4-4 to stop triple option, 172
Teaching, successful, importance of, 23
Three-deep rotation, attacking flat with,
        131-132
    invert coverage, 132
    rotational coverages, 131-132
Three-or-four-deep secondary, using to stop
    passing situation, 115-116, 117
Three-man defensive rushes, 164-165
Three-one prevent zone, 162-163
Throwback, attacking, 221-222
Tight Slot formation, strengths, weaknesses
    and series of, 61
Trap, attacking, 71-72
    stopping, 101
Triple option, attacking, 167-186
    change-up, importance of, 170
    concepts, important, 168-169
    defenses to stop, 171-173
        Eagle-4, 172-173
        Tandem 4-4, 172
        Wide-Tackle 6, 171-172
    execution, principles of, 170-171
    5-4 defense, 174-177
        slanting techniques, 176
        stacking from, 177
        stunt on corner, 175-176
    formation defenses, 170
    offensive plays to be controlled, 169
    other field situation defenses, 185-186
    outside veer, attacking, 184-185
    personnel important factor, 168
    with Pro-4 defense, 177-179
        stunting and slanting, 179
    secondary coverages, defensive,
        183-184

Triple option, attacking (continued)
        veer, stopping, 168-169
        with Split-4 defense, 180-182
            slanting, 182
            stunting, 181-182
Triple option and drop-back pass, 214-215
Two-deep zone, employing in attacking
    deep areas, 159

                        V

Variations of offensive formations, 50-57
    in-the-backfield adjustments, 54-57
    on-the-line adjustments, 51-54

                        W

Wedge block, defensing, 77
Wide formations, offensive, 49-50
Wide-outs and flats, attacking, 115-138
    different coverages, importance of,
        116
    disguising defensive coverages, 128-
        129
    flanker or slot, defensive coverage of
        before offensive snap, 120-
            125
        front alignment, bringing
            defender out from, 125
        new defense, installing, 120
        pre-rotating secondary, 121-
            125
    flat, attacking with four-deep
        secondary, 129-131
        invert coverage, 131
        rotational coverage, 130
    flat, attacking with three-deep rota-
        tion, 131-132
        invert coverage, 132
        rotational coverages, 131-132
    flats, different offensive pass routes
        in, 117-118
    formations, 116-117
    pass routes, offensive, attacking,
        136-138
        flat route, covering, 136-137
        "in routes" from wide receiver,
            138
        "out routes" by wide receiver,
            covering, 138
        seam route, covering, 137
        swing route, covering, 137
    receiver, wide-out, attacking with
        three- and four-deep secondaries,
            133-136
        all zone coverage with one de-
            fender playing man-to-
                man, 136

Wide-outs and flats, attacking *(continued)*
    man underneath coverage with
        deep zone, 134
    one-on-one, man-to-man cover-
        age, 134
    two man-to-man defenders,
        135
    zone underneath coverage with
        deep man-to-man,
        134-135
split end, defensive coverage of before
    offensive snap, 126-128
    front alignment, bringing de-
        fender from, 126
    new defense, installing, 127
    pre-rotating secondary,
        127-128
three- or-four-deep secondary, 115-
    116, 117

Wide-outs and flats, attacking *(continued)*
    wide-outs and flats, attacking with
        different defenses, 118-119
Wide Slot—Split Backfield formation,
    strengths, weaknesses and series of,
    61-62
Wide-Tackle 6 Even-Diamond defense, 44-
    45
Wide-Tackle 6 to stop triple option, 171-172
Wing "T" formation, strengths, weaknesses
    and series of, 58-59
    Wing "T"-Split End, 60-61
Winning Play Sequences in Modern Football,
    204n

Z

Zone coverage, utilizing, 146-148